Ferret

David Balmain

O'REILLY®

Beijing • Cambridge • Farnham • Köln • Paris • Sebastopol • Taipei • Tokyo

Ferret
by David Balmain

Published by O'Reilly Media, Inc., 1005 Gravenstein Highway North, Sebastopol, CA 95472

O'Reilly books may be purchased for educational, business, or sales promotional use. Online editions are also available for most titles (*http://safari.oreilly.com*). For more information, contact our corporate/institutional sales department: 800-998-9938 or *corporate@oreilly.com*.

Editor: Mike Loukides
Production Editor: Sarah Schneider
Proofreader: Sarah Schneider
Indexer: Ellen Troutman Zaig
Cover Designer: Karen Montgomery
Interior Designer: David Futato
Illustrator: Rob Romano

Printing History:
March 2008: First Edition.

This book uses RepKover™, a durable and flexible lay-flat binding.

ISBN: 978-0-596-51940-7

[M]

Table of Contents

Preface

I first became fascinated by information retrieval during my time as a student at the University of Sydney. Back in those days, finding what you wanted on the Web was an art form. I used to have a list of about six or seven search engines that I used every time I had a query and even then I had to page through their results before I found what I was looking for. As the Web exploded it seemed like it was getting harder to find what I was looking for. Then, during my last year at university, I found that more and more I was turning to a single search engine for all my queries and most of the time I didn't even need to click past the first page of results. A newcomer at the time, Google had gone on to demonstrate, through its success, the importance of accurate information retrieval on the Web.

Around that time I was writing a statistical based natural language parser for my honors thesis, so I was no stranger to large-scale text processing. After a few years working as an IT consultant, I was really keen to get back to work on something algorithmically interesting. In 2004, I had left the corporate life to go and train in Judo at the Kodokan in Japan, and I found myself with a little spare time on my hands. I also had a new-found interest in the Ruby programming language, which was perfect for most of the little side projects I was working on except for one thing: it was missing a good information retrieval library. This was the perfect project for me to learn Ruby and to get my hands dirty doing some interesting programming. So I began my first port of the Apache Lucene information retrieval library into Ruby.

As it turns out, Ruby is not the best programming language to write this kind of processor-intensive text processing code. Ferret has evolved since then into one of the fastest search libraries available. It has been through three rewrites and is now written completely in C with Ruby bindings, and the algorithms and file formats have changed significantly from those used in Lucene to improve performance. It is now used in projects all over the world online and offline from large-scale news web sites to legal archive search engines.

From what started out as a side project to learn a new programming language, Ferret has come a long way.

—David Balmain

February 2008

Conventions Used in This Book

The following typographical conventions are used in this book:

Italic
: Indicates new terms, URLs, email addresses, filenames, and file extensions.

`Constant width`
: Used for program listings, as well as within paragraphs to refer to program elements such as variable or function names, databases, datatypes, environment variables, statements, and keywords.

`Constant width bold`
: Shows commands or other text that should be typed literally by the user.

`Constant width italic`
: Shows text that should be replaced with user-supplied values or by values determined by context.

This icon signifies a tip, suggestion, or general note.

This icon indicates a warning or caution.

Using Code Examples

This book is here to help you get your job done. In general, you may use the code in this book in your programs and documentation. You do not need to contact us for permission unless you're reproducing a significant portion of the code. For example, writing a program that uses several chunks of code from this book does not require permission. Selling or distributing a CD-ROM of examples from O'Reilly books does require permission. Answering a question by citing this book and quoting example code does not require permission.

Incorporating a significant amount of example code from this book into your product's documentation does require permission.

We appreciate, but do not require, attribution. An attribution usually includes the title, author, publisher, and ISBN. For example: "*Ferret* by David Balmain. Copyright 2008 O'Reilly Media, Inc., 978-0-596-51940-7."

If you feel your use of code examples falls outside fair use or the permission given above, feel free to contact us at *permissions@oreilly.com*.

Safari® Enabled

When you see a Safari® Enabled icon on the cover of your favorite technology book, that means the book is available online through the O'Reilly Network Safari Bookshelf.

Safari offers a solution that's better than e-books. It's a virtual library that lets you easily search thousands of top tech books, cut and paste code samples, download chapters, and find quick answers when you need the most accurate, current information. Try it for free at *http://safari.oreilly.com*.

How to Contact Us

Please address comments and questions concerning this book to the publisher:

O'Reilly Media, Inc.
1005 Gravenstein Highway North
Sebastopol, CA 95472
800-998-9938 (in the United States or Canada)
707-829-0515 (international or local)
707-829-0104 (fax)

We have a web page for this book, where we list errata, examples, and any additional information. You can access this page at:

http://www.oreilly.com/catalog/9780596519407

To comment or ask technical questions about this book, send email to:

bookquestions@oreilly.com

For more information about our books, conferences, Resource Centers, and the O'Reilly Network, see our web site at:

http://www.oreilly.com

CHAPTER 1

Getting Started

Installing Ferret

First things first: let's get Ferret installed. Thanks to RubyGems, this is pretty easy. If you haven't used RubyGems before, there is a great introduction at the RubyGems web site (*http://docs.rubygems.org/*). If you are on Windows and you used the Ruby One-Click Installer to install Ruby, you'll have everything you need. Other systems, such as Linux or Mac, need to have `make` and a C compiler such as `gcc` to build the extension. Other than that, Ferret comes dependency-free. You simply need to run the `gem install` script:

```
dave$ sudo gem install ferret
```

Once this process successfully completes, you will have Ferret installed on your system. The easiest way to check that everything is working correctly is to open an `irb` session, as shown in Example 1-1.

Example 1-1. irb session

```
dave$ irb -rubygems
>> require 'ferret'                          #=> true
>> index = Ferret::I.new                     #=> #<Ferret::Index:...>
>> index << "Time heals all wounds"          #=> #<Ferret::Index:...>
>> index << "A rolling stone gathers no moss" #=> #<Ferret::Index:...>
>> index << "A stitch in time saves nine"    #=> #<Ferret::Index:...>
>> index << "Look before you leap"           #=> #<Ferret::Index:...>
>> index << "Time and tide wait for no man"  #=> #<Ferret::Index:...>
>> index << "Time wounds all heels"          #=> #<Ferret::Index:...>
>> puts index.search("time")
```

All we've done here is load RubyGems and Ferret, create a new in-memory index, add a few strings to it, and run a search, printing out the results. If everything is working correctly, you will see the results of your search printed out in order of relevance. It doesn't get much simpler than that. `irb` is a great way to play around with Ferret and try out new things. Next, we'll show you how to index all the text files under a particular directory.

A Quick Example: Indexing the Filesystem

With the explosion of the Internet, a huge amount of information has become available to us. But it doesn't matter how much information is available if we can't find what we are looking for. Luckily, companies like Google and Yahoo! have come to the rescue by helping us find the information we need with their search engines.

More recently, the same thing has been happening on our personal computers. More and more of our personal lives are being stored on hard drives—everything from work documents and email to multimedia files and family photos. Carefully categorizing all this data and scanning through large hierarchies of folders just doesn't cut it anymore. We need a fast way to access the data we need. Presently, some of the tools commonly used for this task, such as the built-in search in Windows, leave a lot to be desired. Spotlight on OS X is much closer to what we need.

By the end of this book, you'll have built a search application that will make searching your hard drive as easy as searching the Web. In this section, we start with plain old text files. Let's begin by writing a command-line indexing program that takes two arguments: the name of the directory we want to index, and the name of the directory in which the index will be stored. Take a look at Example 1-2.

Example 1-2. index.rb

```
#!/usr/bin/env ruby
require 'rubygems'
require 'ferret'
require 'fileutils'
include Ferret
include Ferret::Index

def usage(message = nil)
  puts message if message
  puts "ruby #{File.basename(__FILE__)} <data dir> <index dir>"
  exit(1)
end

usage() if ARGV.size != 2
usage("Directory '#{ARGV[0]}' doesn't exist.") unless File.directory?(ARGV[0])
$data_dir, $index_dir = ARGV
begin
  FileUtils.mkdir_p($index_dir)
rescue
  usage("Can't create index directory '#$index_dir'.")
```

```
20 end
21
22 index = Index.new(:path => $index_dir,
23                   :create => true)
24
25 Dir["#$data_dir/**/*.txt"].each do |file_name|
26   index << {:file_name => file_name, :content => File.read(file_name)}
27 end
28 index.optimize()
29 index.close()
```

Most of this code is for command-line argument handling and can be safely skimmed over. The interesting part of the code begins on line 22. This is where we create the index. The `:path` parameter clearly specifies where you want to store the index. Setting the `:create` parameter to `true` tells Ferret to create a new index in the specified directory. Any index already residing in the specified directory will be overwritten, so be careful when setting `:create` to `true`. We saw earlier that we can add simple `Strings` to an index. This time we use a `Hash`, as we want each document to have two fields.

Once the index is created, we need to add documents to it. Line 25 simply scans a directory tree for all text files. Line 26 is where most of the action is happening. Since we can add simple `Strings` to an index, we use a `Hash` because we want each document to have two fields: a `:file_name` field and a `:content` field. Later, we'll learn about the `Document` class, which lets us assign weightings (or boosts, as they are known in Ferret) to *documents* and *fields*.

The `Index#optimize` method is called on line 28. This method optimizes the index for searching, and it is a good idea to call it whenever you do a batch indexing.[*] On the following line, we close the index. `Index#close` will make sure that any data held in RAM is flushed to the index. It then commits the index and closes any locks that the `Index` object might be holding on the index.

Locking Problems

It is vitally important to close your index when you have finished with it, or you could run into locking errors later on. This is one of the largest causes of error in Ferret. We'll cover locking issues in the "Index Locking and Concurrency Issues" section in Chapter 3.

To make things a little easier, you can pass a block to the `Index.new` method, as you would to `File.open`, so that the index is automatically closed when you have finished with it:

[*] When doing incremental indexing, as you might do in a Rails application, it is better not to call the `optimize` method. You'll learn more about this in the "Optimizing the Index" section in Chapter 3.

```
Ferret::Index::Index.new(:path => 'path/to/index') do |index|
  documents.each {|doc| index << doc}
  index.search_each(query) {|id, score| puts "#{score} #{index[id].load}"}
end
```

Creating an index is now simply a matter of running the indexer from the command line:

```
dave$ ruby index.rb index_dir/ text_files/
```

Now that we have an index, we need to be able to search it. That is why we built it, after all. The search code is as simple as the indexing code; take a look at Example 1-3.

Example 1-3. search.rb

```
#!/usr/bin/env ruby
require 'rubygems'
require 'ferret'
require 'fileutils'
include Ferret
include Ferret::Index

def usage(message = nil)
  puts message if message
  puts "ruby #{File.basename(__FILE__)} <index dir> <search phrase>"
  exit(1)
end

usage() if ARGV.size != 2
usage("Index '#{ARGV[0]}' doesn't exist.") unless File.directory?(ARGV[0])
$index_dir, $search_phrase = ARGV

index = Index.new(:path => $index_dir)

results = []
total_hits = index.search_each($search_phrase) do |doc_id, score|
  results << "  #{score} - #{index[doc_id][:file_name]}"
end

puts "#{total_hits} matched your query:\n" + results.join("\n")

index.close()
```

Document IDs in Ferret

In Ferret, documents are referenced by document IDs. You can think of a Ferret index as an array of documents indexed from 0. As each new document is added to an index, it is assigned the next available document ID. However, it is important to note that the document ID does not remain consistent for the life of a document in the index. As documents are updated and deleted from the index and index segments are merged and optimized, document IDs will change.

On line 21 we simply write the results to a string. You can use the document ID to access the index; the document itself acts like a `Hash` object. If you would like to build an index of a large number of text files, check out Project Gutenberg (*http://www.gutenberg.org/*). Go ahead and try out the search script:

```
dave$ ruby search.rb index_dir/ "Moby Dick"
```

Summary

So far we've met the `Index` class. This class is just a convenient, easy-to-use interface to the rest of the Ferret API. It does most of the hard work for you, such as parsing queries and keeping track of the `IndexReader` and `IndexWriter` classes behind the scenes, or knowing when to commit the index so that your search is always on the latest version of the index. There is a lot more that you can do with the `Index` class, and in most cases it will be all you need. But if you really want to take full advantage of all Ferret has to offer, you'll need to find out what is going on behind the scenes. In Chapter 2, we'll learn more about how indexing actually works and how to configure the index for your application.

CHAPTER 2
Indexing

When you are indexing with Ferret, you need to know about the following classes:

- `Ferret::Store::Directory`
- `Ferret::Index::FieldInfo`
- `Ferret::Index::FieldInfos`
- `Ferret::Field`
- `Ferret::Document`
- `Ferret::Index::IndexWriter`
- `Ferret::Index::IndexReader`

We will discuss each of these classes in this chapter. We'll begin by discussing index storage. This involves looking at the two implementations of the `Directory` class: `RAMDirectory` and `FSDirectory`. After that, we'll look at the building blocks of the Ferret index—the `Field` and `Document` classes—and we'll discuss document and field boosting. We'll then look at setting up the index. This involves using the `FieldInfo` and `FieldInfos` class and is probably the most important topic in this chapter. Finally, we'll discuss how the actual indexing process works, at which time you'll learn when to use the `IndexReader` and `IndexWriter` classes. Readers should pay special attention to the "Index Locking and Concurrency Issues" section in Chapter 3, as it seems to be the biggest problem area for new users in Ferret.

Index Storage

Ferret indexes are stored in a `Ferret::Store::Directory`. `Directory` is an abstract class that specifies how an index should be stored. Ferret comes packaged with two implementations of the `Directory` class: `Ferret::Store::FSDirectory` for storing the index on the filesystem, and

Ferret::Store::RAMDirectory for storing an index in memory. You've used both of these classes already: RAMDirectory in Example 1-1 and FSDirectory in Examples 1-2 and 1-3. The Index class hides all the details, but when you pass a :path parameter to Index.new, an FSDirectory is used; otherwise, a RAMDirectory is used.

Most of the time, you will persist your index to the filesystem, so you'll be using FSDirectory. For the most part, RAMDirectory is used internally during indexing. There are times, however, when RAMDirectory will come in handy. It is a little faster than FSDirectory, so if you have a small index that will fit in your available memory and you need a really fast search, you might choose to use a RAMDirectory. You can even load an existing filesystem index into a RAMDirectory:

```
dir = RAMDirectory.new(FSDirectory.new('path/to/index'))
```

RAMDirectory is most beneficial during testing. Each unit test can create a new in-memory index, which is automatically cleaned up at the end of the test.

Documents, Fields, and Boosts

Documents

The best way to think of an index is as a searchable array of *documents*. A Ferret document is a collection of *fields* representing a chunk of data that you want to make searchable. Whether that chunk of data is a database row, a Word document, or an MP3 file doesn't matter. They are all just documents to Ferret. A Ferret document can be represented by the Ferret::Document class. This class extends Ruby's Hash class, adding only a boost attribute. In fact, as you saw in Example 1-2, documents can also be Hashes, where the key is the name of the field and the value is the data stored in the field.

Ferret Field Names

Field names should always be represented by :symbols rather than strings. That is, you should add fields like this:

```
index << {:title => "Tom Sawyer", :author => "Mark Twain"}
```

Not like this:

```
index << {"title" => "Tom Sawyer", "author" => "Mark Twain"}
```

The term "document" can be quite confusing. We often need to talk about the idea of a document in an index that is implemented by the Document class. A document can represent a PDF or a text document, or it can represent something like a movie or a product. Make note of the formatting we use to distinguish documents from the `Document` class.

Earlier we mentioned that `Documents` have a `boost` attribute, but we didn't say what `boost` was for. The `boost` attribute gives a document a higher weighting in the results of a search. By using the `boost` attribute, you can make more important documents appear higher in the search results. The default `boost` value is 1.0, so if you have a document that you consider to be important, you might set its `boost` to 100.0. Another document that you consider less important might have its `boost` set to 0.0001.

To illustrate this point, let's say you have an online bookstore that sells a number of books on fishing. If one of your users comes along and submits a query with the term "fishing", you might show a list of the top 10 books found. But how do you rate the top 10? By default, Ferret returns the books in which the term "fishing" appears most frequently, relative to the size of the document. However, just having a high occurrence of the term "fishing" doesn't necessarily make the book a great book on fishing. It would be better if you could *boost* the fishing books that have good reviews or are highly rated, so they are more likely to appear at the top of the search results, and that is what the `boost` attribute is for:

```
doc = Document.new(book.rating)
doc[:title] = book.title
doc[:content] = book.content
index << doc
```

Fields

Whereas documents are represented by `Hashes`, *fields* can be represented by `Strings` or `Arrays` of `Strings`. More often than not, you'll use a `String` to represent the data in a field, but there are times when it makes more sense to use an `Array`. Consider the situation where you want a field to hold a list of the document's tags. You can do it like this:

```
index << {:title => "Ferret", :tags => ["ruby", "gem", "search library"]}
```

We could have joined the tags into a single string separated by spaces, but then we wouldn't have known that "search library" was a single tag rather than two separate tags.

Like documents, fields also have their own `Ferret::Field` class that extends `Array` by adding a `boost` attribute. When you set the boost on a `Field`, you give the terms in that field a higher or lower weighting compared to terms in other fields, but only for that particular document. Note that this boost applies to one document only. It may be tempting, for example, to boost all documents' :title fields in this way, but the better approach is to set the default boost for the :title field when you set up the index. You'll learn how to do this in the next section ("Boosts").

Imagine you have a movie database that lets you search by title or subject. You don't really need to boost one movie's :title field over another's, since searches on the :title field are mostly going to be searches for exact titles. However, you might want to boost the :subject field by rating. If you search for boxing movies, you probably want *Raging Bull* to rank higher than *Rocky IV*. So you could create the movie document like this:

```
index << {:title => movie.title,
          :subject => Field.new(movie.keywords, movie.rating)}
```

Or like this:

```
doc = Document.new()
doc[:title] = movie.title
doc[:subject] = Field.new(movie.keywords, movie.rating)
index << doc
```

Why don't we use a single Document and Field class? Why does Ferret need to be able to accept Hashes and Arrays? Basically, it's because Hashes and Arrays are the staple data structures in Ruby, and every Ruby programmer knows how to use them. This makes Ferret easier to use and lowers the barrier of entry. In most cases you won't need to add boosts to individual documents or fields, and you should stick to using Hashes rather than Documents.

Here is a summary of all the ways you can add a document to an index:

```
index << {:title => "Tom Sawyer", :author => "Mark Twain"}
index << {:file_name => "ferret.jpg", :tags => ["ferret", "logo"]}
index << {:product_name => Field.new("ipod", 10.0), :color => "black"}
doc = Document.new(100.0) # set boost to 100.0
doc[:title] = "Shawshank Redemption"
doc[:actors] = ["Tim Robbins", "Morgan Freeman"]
doc[:subject] = Field.new(["jail", "prison", "friendship"])
index << doc
```

Ferret Fields Versus Apache Lucene Fields

If you have used Apache Lucene or Ferret prior to version 0.10.0, you might be surprised to see that properties aren't available in Ferret's field object. In previous versions of Ferret, you could specify how the indexer treats each field in the document when it is added to the index. For example, you could specify that a :title field gets stored, even though the same :title field in another document doesn't get stored. This behavior just complicates the indexer and makes the API a lot uglier, while not really adding much in terms of functionality. It is rare that anyone wants a particular field to have differing properties for each document. Ferret was able to gain major performance improvements by removing this feature.

In Ferret, you decide beforehand which properties you want a field to have, just as you would the columns of a database. This doesn't mean you can't dynamically create new fields as you go. It just means that once you do create a field, the properties it starts with are the properties it keeps for the life of the index.

Boosts

If you'd like to forget about using the `Document` and `Field` classes, you can easily add a `boost` attribute to any class you want using the `Ferret::BoostMixin`. Here we add it to `Hash`, `Array`, and `String`:

```
class String
  include Ferret::BoostMixin
end
class Array
  include Ferret::BoostMixin
end
class Hash
  include Ferret::BoostMixin
end
```

So, what kind of `boost` values should you use to boost your documents? `Boost` values are converted from a `Float` value into a single byte for storage in the index, so there will be some roundoff error in the usage of boost values. If you want to boost one field over another, use multiple differences 2–10 times rather than small percentage differences.

Setting Up the Index

We now know that the index is made up of documents, which, in turn, are made up of fields. What happens to the fields when they are added to the index? Are they all treated equally? By default, the answer is yes: each field is created with the same properties. But this is not always desirable. For example, Ferret stores all the text in all the fields unmodified by default. If you are indexing data from a database, this may not be necessary. Since you are already storing the data in the database, it is often pointless to store it in the Ferret index as well.*

* To add query result highlighting to your application, store the fields you want to highlight, even if they are stored elsewhere (like in a database). Or you could implement your own highlighter.

FieldInfo

Each field in a Ferret index has its properties defined in a `Ferret::Index::FieldInfo` object. A `FieldInfo` is an immutable class with the following properties:

- `name`
- `boost`
- `stored?`
- `compressed?`
- `indexed?`
- `tokenized?`
- `omit_norms?`
- `store_term_vectors?`
- `store_positions?`
- `store_offsets?`

The `FieldInfo#name` property is a symbol used to match the `FieldInfo` object with a field in a document. `FieldInfo#boost` is the default boost that is given to each instance of the field when it is added to the index. This is where, for example, you would boost the `:title` field if you wanted it to have more weight in the search results than the `:content` field. The default value for `#boost` is 1.0.

The rest of these properties can be divided into three groups: *store*, *index*, and *term_vector*. These are the other parameters you can use to instantiate a new `FieldInfo` object. For example:

```
field_info = FieldInfo.new(:title,
                           :default_boost => 20,
                           :store => :yes,
                           :index => :untokenized,
                           :term_vector => :no)
```

:store

Fields in Ferret can be stored or unstored. You should store fields that you want to retrieve after a search. For example, you would probably store a file URL if you are indexing your filesystem, or the ID (primary key) of a database table row when indexing a database table. You can also use a Ferret index like a database, storing all of your data in it. If you want to add highlighting to your search results, you need to store the fields you want to highlight. If a field is stored, it can also be compressed. This is useful when storing large documents in the index and disk space becomes an issue. It makes no sense to have a field that is both unstored and compressed. Table 2-1 shows the three options for the `:store` parameter.

Table 2-1. :store options

Options	Stored?	Compressed?
`:no`	`false`	`false`
`:yes`[a]	`true`	`false`
`:compressed`	`true`	`true`

[a] Boldface signifies a default value.

The default value for `:store` is `:yes`.

:index

Fields can optionally be indexed. Indexing is the process of making fields searchable, so most of the time you want your fields to be indexed. There are certain times when you won't want or need a field to be searchable. You could, if you wanted to, store image files in a Ferret index; in this case, you wouldn't want the image data itself to be indexed.

You may think that you are never going to want to search the `:id` field when you are indexing data from a Rails database. After all, you can use the database for that, right? Although it is clear that your users are not going to search this field, you need to make sure the `:id` field is indexed so that an updated row in the database can be replicated in the index. That is to say, the `:id` field needs to be indexed so that the database row can be associated with the corresponding document in the index.

After you decide to index a field, you then need to decide if you want to tokenize the field. Tokenizing is the process of splitting up the field's data into searchable terms. You should tokenize any fields that should be included in a full text search: a `:content` field, for example. On the other hand, any field that you use as a document key should be left untokenized. For example, you probably won't want to tokenize file URLs, and you definitely won't want to tokenize database IDs.

The `:index` parameter handles one other option: whether or not you want to omit the *norms* file. The norms file stores the `boost` value and normalization factor for each field in the index. Each norm value takes up 1 byte, so if you have 10,000 documents and 100 indexed fields, your norms files will take up (100 × 10,000) = 1,000,000 bytes. That's not much disk space, but these files actually get read into memory when you open an index for searching. It may be worth your while to omit the norms files when they are not necessary. If you are not boosting the field and it is untokenized, you may as well omit the norms.

That leaves you with the `:index` parameter options shown in Table 2-2.

Table 2-2. :index options

Options	Indexed?	Tokenized?	omit_norms?
`:no`	`false`	`false`	`false`
`:yes`	`true`	`true`	`false`
`:untokenized`	`true`	`false`	`false`
`:yes_omit_norms`	`true`	`true`	`true`
`:untokenized_omit_norms`	`true`	`false`	`true`

The default value for `:index` is `:yes`.

:term_vector

For each document field, the term vector stores its list of terms and the frequency of each of those terms in the document. You can optionally store the positions and offsets of each of the terms. The positions are the term indexes of each instance of a term in the field. For example, in the phrase "the quick brown fox", the word "quick" has a position of 1 (indexing from 0). The offsets are the byte offsets of the start and end of each instance of the terms in the field. So the phrase "quick" has start and end offsets of 4 and 9.

You will need to store term vectors with positions and offsets to add highlighting to your application. You'll find out more about this in the "Highlighting Query Results" section in Chapter 4. So this leaves us with the `:term_vector` parameter options shown in Table 2-3.

Table 2-3. :term_vector options

Options	store_term_vector?	store_positions?	store_offsets?
`:no`	`false`	`false`	`false`
`:yes`	`true`	`false`	`false`
`:with_positions`	`true`	`true`	`false`
`:with_offsets`	`true`	`false`	`true`
`:with_positions_offsets`	`true`	`true`	`true`

The default value for `:term_vector` is `:with_positions_offsets`.

Before we show you any more examples of how to create a `FieldInfo` object, let's see how they all fit together with the `FieldInfos` class.

FieldInfos

Every Ferret index has a `Ferret::Index::FieldInfos` object. This object is a dictionary of `FieldInfo` objects, one for each field in the index. It has default values for the parameters `:store`, `:index`, and `:term_vector`, so it can create new `FieldInfo` objects whenever an unknown field is encountered. So, the initializer for a `FieldInfos` class looks a lot like the initializer for `FieldInfo`. The setup of `FieldInfos` is pretty easy and is best illustrated with an example:

```
field_infos = FieldInfos.new(:store => :yes,
                             :index => :yes,
                             :term_vector => :no)

field_infos << FieldInfo.new(:id,
                             :index => :untokenized,
                             :term_vector => :no)
field_infos << FieldInfo.new(:title,
                             :default_boost => 20.0,
                             :term_vector => :no)
field_infos << FieldInfo.new(:content,
                             :term_vector => :with_positions_offsets)
```

Each of the `FieldInfo` objects inherits the default values from `FieldInfo`, unless otherwise specified. Sometimes, however, you want to use the default values set in the `FieldInfos` class. To do this, you need to use the `FieldInfos::add_field` method. The following example is equivalent to the previous one:

```
field_infos = FieldInfos.new(:term_vector => :no)

field_infos.add_field(:id,      :index => :untokenized)
field_infos.add_field(:title,   :default_boost => 20.0)
field_infos.add_field(:content, :term_vector => :with_positions_offsets)
```

Many developers like to read this kind of information from configuration files. Ferret has support for YAML (YAML Ain't Markup Language) files. We could achieve the above configuration with the file in Example 2-1.

Example 2-1. ferret.yml

```
default:
  store: :yes
  index: :yes
  term_vector: :no

fields:
  id:
    index: :untokenized
    term_vector: :no

  title:
    boost: 20.0
```

```
    term_vector: :no

  content:
    term_vector: :with_positions_offsets
```

To load the YAML file, use the `FieldInfos.load` method:

```
field_infos = FieldInfos.load(File.read("examples/ferret.yml"))
```

After we have set up the `FieldInfos` object, we can use it to initialize a new index. Simply pass it as the `:field_infos` parameter when you instantiate a `Ferret::Index::Index` (or `Ferret::Index::IndexWriter`) object:

```
Ferret::Index::Index.new(:path => "path/to/index",
                         :field_infos => field_infos,
                         :create => true)
```

Note that we set `:create` to `true`. If you pass a `:field_infos` parameter to an existing index, it will be ignored unless you set `:create` to `true`. In this case, the old index will be overwritten. To add new fields to an existing index, you open the index with an `Index` (or `IndexWriter`) and add fields to its `field_infos` attribute:

```
index = Ferret::Index::Index.new(:path => "path/to/index")
index.field_infos.add_field(:created_on,
                            :index => :untokenized,
                            :term_vector => :no)
```

Basic Indexing Operations

Now that you have the index set up, you are ready to start the indexing process. Ferret allows two *write* operations on an index: *add* and *delete*. By combining these two operations, you can perform an *update* operation, which you'll also learn about in this section, as well as retrieving documents from the index. In this section you'll also get an informal introduction to the `Ferret::Index::IndexReader` and `Ferret::Index::IndexWriter` classes through the explanations and examples. You'll learn more about these two classes in Chapter 3.

Add

Adding documents to the index is done with the aptly named `IndexWriter` class. You've already seen how to add documents using the `Index` class; if you look under the covers, you'll find that the `Index` object is just using an `IndexWriter` to write documents to the index:

```
index_writer = IndexWriter.new(:path => 'path/to/index')

documents.each {|doc| index_writer.add_document(doc) }
```

```
index_writer.commit()
```

Notice the `commit` method at the end. None of the changes you make to an index through an `IndexWriter` are guaranteed to be applied until you call either `commit`, `optimize`, or `close`. The `commit` method simply applies all changes to the index, leaving the `IndexWriter` open. `close` does the same thing, then closes the `IndexWriter`. `optimize` is like `commit` in that it commits all changes, leaving the `IndexWriter` open for more index modifications. However, it also optimizes the index for searching. This process can be quite resource-intensive and should be called sparingly, usually after running a batch indexing process or once a day as a cron process.

Get

Once there are documents in the index, you need to be able to retrieve them again. To retrieve documents, use an `IndexReader`:

```
doc = index_reader.get_document(doc_id)
```

You can think of an index as an array of documents and, in fact, you can reference the index just as you would an array:

```
# Get the 6th document in the index
doc = index_reader[5]

# Get the 2nd last document in the index
doc = index_reader[-2]

# Get documents 5 to 10
docs = index_reader[5..10]
```

Delete

This is where things start to get a little confusing. You can use `IndexWriter` to delete documents as you would expect. But you can also use `IndexReader` to delete documents. Both `delete` methods work in slightly different ways. We'll start with `IndexReader#delete`. It may seem a little counterintuitive that a "reader" class can modify the index, but it makes sense when you think about how the index works. We mentioned that Ferret *document IDs* are variable and can change between index commits. Let's imagine that we want to delete all documents with a `:create_date` field older than a certain date. We'd need to use an `IndexReader` to find the document IDs of the documents we wish to delete. Use an `IndexReader` to delete by document ID:

```
index_reader.delete(doc_id)
```

The `IndexReader#delete` method is flexible enough to cover your deletion needs. However, there is a problem with using an `IndexReader` to delete documents. When you open an `IndexWriter`, it obtains a write lock on the index. When you call `IndexReader`'s `delete` method, it tries to do the same, so you will get a locking error if you try to add and delete documents at the same time. To solve this problem, close the `IndexWriter` every time you want to delete a document, then commit the `IndexReader` and open a new `IndexWriter` when you are ready to add another document. It's just as annoying as it sounds. To solve this problem, `IndexWriter` now has its own `delete` method, too. The catch is, it doesn't work in quite the same way as `IndexReader#delete`. Instead of using a *document ID* to identify the document, you give `IndexWriter#delete` a *field* and *term*:

```
index_writer.delete(:path, "/path/to/file")
```

This statement deletes all documents with the field `:path` equal to `"/path/to/file"`. The term should be a uniquely identifying key for the document (like a primary key in a database). Using a unique term ensures that only one document is deleted each time `Index#delete` is called. If the term isn't unique in the index, multiple documents are deleted. This method is especially useful when updating documents.

Update

There is no `update` method in the `IndexWriter` class (although `Index` does supply one), so you need to implement it yourself. The easiest way to implement `update` is to make sure every *document* in the index has one field that acts as a uniquely identifying key. For example, if you are indexing a model from a Rails application, you would use the `:id` field:

```
index_writer.delete(:id, doc[:id])
index_writer.add_document(doc)
```

The `Index` class makes this even easier. Just specify a `:key` when you instantiate the index, and old documents will automatically be deleted whenever you add a new document with an existing key. So our Rails example would look like this:

```
index = Ferret::I.new(:key => :id,
                      :path => 'path/to/index')

# ... and then later simply add documents and old ones will be replaced
index << doc
```

Indexing Non-String Datatypes

So far, we've only really talked about adding strings to the index. As far as Ferret is concerned, every field is a string. But sometimes we want to index other datatypes, such as numbers and dates. We're going to take a moment to talk about best practices when indexing non-string datatypes, specifically storing special datatypes in their own field. We won't mention how to handle numbers or dates within a larger string field (like in the string *The 39 Steps*). You'll learn more about text-field analysis in Chapter 5.

Number Fields

Indexing number fields is relatively straightforward. You don't even need to convert them to strings when you add them to the document. However, you do need to think about how you set up the field. Make sure it is *untokenized*, as some `Analyzers` will strip all numbers and you'll end up with an empty field:

```
index << {:product => "widget", :price => 24.95, :weight => 2400}
```

The one exception is when you want to run range queries on a number field. For example, you may want to submit a query for all products between $5.00 and $25.00 or for all products that weigh less than 500 grams. In Ferret, the `RangeQuery` sorts fields lexicographically, so while 200 comes before 500, 70 comes after 500. To fix this, pad the numbers to a fixed width by prepending zeros. So instead of adding 5, 70, and 200, you would add 0005, 0070, and 0200, and instead of adding 3.45 and 101.95, you would add 0003.45 and 0101.95. This is pretty easy using Ruby's printf-like notation:

```
index << {:product => "widget",
          :price => "%06.2f" % 24.95,
          :weight => "%04d" % 2400}
```

In the "Custom Analysis" section in Chapter 5, we'll show you how to automate this in an `Analyzer` so that you no longer need to think about it when adding documents.

Date Fields

As with numbers fields, you can add `Times` to a document; the time is converted to a `String` using its `to_s` method when it is added to the index:

```
index << {:id => "0", :create_date => Time.new}
```

Again, be sure to set the field type to *untokenized*. When it comes to dates, though, they can be written in so many different formats that it's worth taking some time to consider which format to use. Like numbers, dates are common in range queries, so you should try to pick a date format that is ordered correctly when sorted lexicographically. Any of the following will work, so pick one and stick to it:

```
t = Time.now
index << {:id => "0", :date => t.strftime("%Y%m%d")}        # 20060725
index << {:id => "1", :date => t.strftime("%Y/%m/%d")}      # 2006/07/25
index << {:id => "2", :date => t.strftime("%Y-%m-%d")}      # 2006-07-25
index << {:id => "3", :date => t.strftime("%Y%m%d%H%M")}    # 200607251445
index << {:id => "4", :date => t.strftime("%Y-%m-%d %H:%M")}# 2006-07-25
   14:45
```

We highly recommend using the "%Y%m%d" format if you plan to sort by this field, as it makes it possible to perform an integer sort rather than a string sort. Integer sorts are much faster and use a fraction of the memory.

Whichever format you decide to use, you'll be using that format when you type search queries. That is to say, you'll have to type dates using that format into your queries. Also, make sure you use the minimum precision necessary. By adding the hour to the date format, you will have potentially 24 times the number of unique date terms in your index. All of these terms must be iterated through whenever you search the date field. For example, let's say we have the times "20060101-10:13", "20060101-13:45", "20060101-23:33", and "20060102-01:01". If we reduced the precision to daily, we'd reduce the number of terms to two: "20060101", "20060102". Reduce the precision to monthly and we have the single term "200601". The implications of this on a larger database should be clear.

Sort Fields

Ferret allows you to sort search results, not only by score, but also by field values. You'll learn more about sorting your result sets in the "Sorting Search Results" section in Chapter 4. For now, let's consider how the fields that you want your results to be sorted in are set up. Ferret includes four field sort implementations: integer, float, byte, and string. (There is also an `auto` field sort that chooses one of `integer`, `float`, or `string`, but we won't worry about that for now.)

When you sort your search results the first time, Ferret runs through all the terms in the sorted fields and caches the parsed field values for each document in the index. So if we are sorting a `:weight` field by integer, it runs through every term in the `:weight` field, parses it into an integer, and records all the documents in which that term occurs. To make a field sortable, it must be indexed. If the field is tokenized, the sorting algorithm won't know which term in the field to use, so the field should also be untokenized.

> The exception to this rule is when you implement a custom analyzer that only returns one token per field. This can be a handy way to pad numbers to fixed width, as you'll see in the "Custom Analysis" section in Chapter 5.

There is no need to store the field or include any term vectors, so you will usually set up your sortable fields like this:

```
sortable_field = FieldInfo.new(:sortable_field,
                               :store => :no,
                               :index => :untokenized,
                               :term_vector => :no)
```

If you want to make a number field sortable, there is no need to pad it, but padding won't hurt, and it is essential if you also want to run range queries on that field. You just need to make sure that every value in that field can be parsed into a number (either an integer or a float).

Dates, again, are a tricky issue. If you can use any of the formats from the previous section, a string sort will work just fine. However, string sorts can be quite expensive and it would be better to use an integer sort. You can do this by storing the date in the YYYYMMDD (`"%Y%m%d"`) format, which is easily parsed into an integer.

Summary

You now know how to set up an index, including what kinds of properties are available for each field. We also covered how to set up fields for indexing different datatypes, such as numbers and dates, as well as how to setup a field for sorting. You've learned about document and field boosting, and how to perform the basic operations `add`, `get`, `update`, and `delete` on a Ferret index. That pretty much covers everything you need to know about indexing with Ferret.

Chapter 3 takes indexing to the next level. You'll learn more about how the indexing process works and how to tune your index to get the best possible performance from it. If performance is not a concern for you—and Ferret is usually fast enough out of the box—you can probably skip most of the next chapter. But everyone should carefully read the "Index Locking and Concurrency Issues" section.

CHAPTER 3

Advanced Indexing

So far, we've taken a black-box approach to Ferret. This chapter explains what is really going on during indexing and, in the process, explains how to tune your index for maximum performance. We conclude by explaining how locking works. It is crucial that you understand this, particularly if you want to run Ferret in a multithreaded or multiprocess environment.

How the Indexing Process Works

We are now going to show how a source document—such as an HTML document from the Web, a row from a database, or an image from your personal image collection—becomes a Ferret document stored in the index. Ferret is agnostic about the source document's type. It doesn't matter whether you are indexing an MP3 file, a text document, or your store's product, Ferret treats it as a collection of string fields. So, the first step is to turn source documents into `Documents`. This is pretty easy with plain-text documents. With other text document types, such as PDF or HTML, you'll need to write a parser/reader that extracts the searchable text from the documents. For an image file, you might have a parser that extracts EXIF tags. Database rows usually map pretty easily to `Documents`. See Chapter 6 for a framework for doing exactly this.

Once you have a `Document`, you add it to an `IndexWriter`. This is where the magic begins. The `Document`'s fields are passed through an analyzer (if they are set to be tokenized) that breaks up the fields into searchable tokens however it sees fit (see Chapter 5 for more information). Once the `Document` has passed through the analyzer, it is buffered until the `IndexWriter` is ready to write a new segment to the index. Exactly how many documents are buffered depends on the `IndexWriter`'s `:max_buffered_docs` and `:max_buffer_memory` parameters, which are discussed in the "Indexing Parameters" section later in this chapter.

When an `IndexWriter` hits its limit for the maximum number of buffered documents, or when it is committed, it writes the buffered documents to a

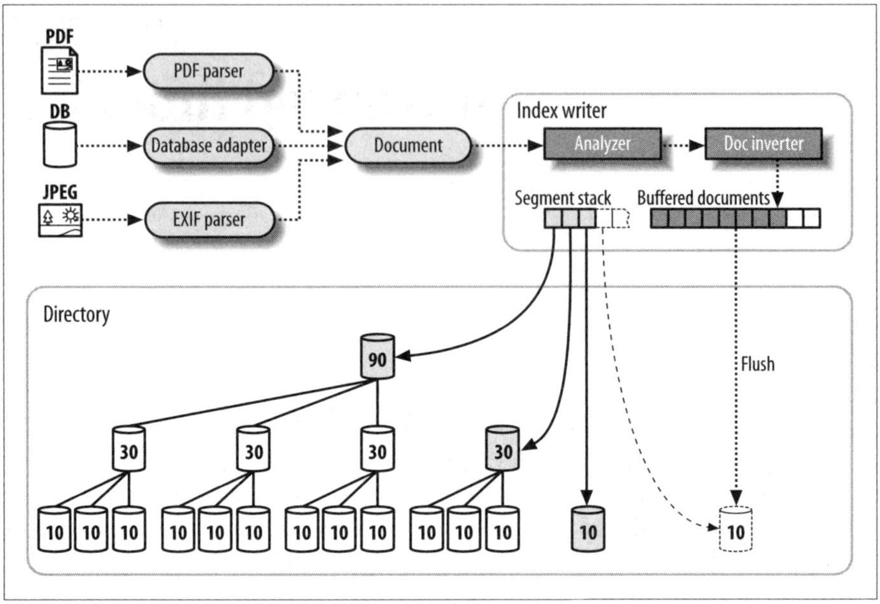

Figure 3-1. Indexing flow chart

segment in the `Directory`. In Figure 3-1, the `IndexWriter` buffers 10 documents before writing them as a segment. As segments are written to the index, the `IndexWriter` maintains a segment stack. Each time a segment is pushed onto the stack, the `IndexWriter` checks to see if there are `:merge_factor` segments on top of the stack that are all the same size. If there are, they are popped off the stack, merged, the merged segment is pushed back onto the stack, and the process is repeated. In Figure 3-1, the merge factor is set to 3, so if there are three 10-document segments on top of the stack, they are merged into one 30-document segment. Likewise, three 30-document segments are merged into one 90-document segment, and so on.

> `:merge_factor` is the minimum number of segments of the same size that must exist before they are merged. See the ":merge_factor" section later in this chapter.

This process is designed to keep the frequency of segment merges to a minimum for the sake of indexing speed, while still keeping the number of segments to be searched small enough so that the index can be search quickly.

Tuning Indexing Performance

Ferret's indexing performance is lightning-fast out of the box, so you're justified in wondering whether you need to know how to make Ferret even faster. In most cases, you won't need Ferret to go any faster than it already does. But if you are indexing gigabytes rather than megabytes and the indexing process is taking hours rather than seconds, you need to know how to push Ferret to its limits.

In-Memory Indexing

People who have used Lucene or earlier versions of Ferret might try to improve indexing speed by indexing to a `RAMDirectory` and then flushing the `RAMDirectory` to disk. That trick is now pointless; Ferret automatically indexes as many documents as it can in memory before flushing them to the `Directory`. You can ensure that all the indexing is done in memory by setting the parameters `:max_buffered_docs` and `:max_buffer_memory` to sufficiently large quantities.

Indexing Parameters

The indexing process is regulated by the parameters, shown with their defaults in Table 3-1.

Table 3-1. Index parameters

Parameter	Default	Short description
`:max_buffer_memory`	16 Mb	The maximum memory used by the `IndexWriter` before buffered documents are flushed to the index
`:chunk_size`	1 Mb	The size of the memory chunks allocated to the memory pool during indexing
`:merge_factor`	10	The minimum number of similar sized segments needed to trigger a merge
`:max_buffered_docs`	10,000	The maximum number of documents that will be buffered by the `IndexWriter` before they are flushed to the index
`:max_merge_docs`	Infinite	The maximum number of documents that will be merged into a single segment
`:max_field_length`	10,000	The maximum number of terms from any field that will be added to the index
`:use_compound_file`	`true`	Specifies whether or not to write the index in compound file format
`:index_skip_interval`	128	The skip interval between terms in the term dictionary
`:doc_skip_interval`	16	The skip interval between document IDs in the term dictionary

In this section, we will go through each of these parameters in turn and explain the effects they have on the indexing processes. In some cases, the parameters will also affect search speed, so that will also be discussed.

:max_buffer_memory and :chunk_size

The `:max_buffer_memory` and `:chunk_size` parameters go hand in hand. These parameters regulate how memory is allocated by the indexing process, so use them with care. `:max_buffer_memory` defines how much memory can be used by the indexing process. By default it is set to 16 Mb, but you can set it as high as your system will allow.

> **Ferret Indexing Memory Usage**
>
> The indexing process can go over the limit set by `:max_buffer_memory`. To calculate possible memory usage, add three times the size of the largest document you are adding to the index plus `:max_buffer_memory`. So, if the maximum document size is 10 Mb and `:max_buffer_memory` is set to 256 Mb, the indexing process could use up to 256 + 3 × 10 = 286 Mb memory.

When you set `:max_buffer_memory` to a large value like 512 Mb, you don't want the `IndexWriter`, so allocate 512 Mb at once. The `:chunk_size` parameter specifies the size of the memory chunks that are allocated to the memory pool.

`:max_buffer_memory` has the largest effect on indexing speed of all indexing parameters. It should be the first parameter you play with when tuning your indexer. `:chunk_size` won't have much affect at all and can usually be left at 1 Mb.

:merge_factor

This parameter specifies how many segments of a certain size need to exist on the top of the segment stack before they are merged. A low merge factor such as 2 or 3 causes a high number of merges, which slows down indexing, but it also means fewer segments, which is great for searching. A high merge factor such as 100 means that segments are merged very rarely, which should improve indexing speed; the downside is there will be a large number of segments in the index and searching will be slow. If you choose a merge factor that is too large, you will end up with too many segments, possibly hitting your operating system's limit for the number of open files.

:max_buffered_docs

This parameter specifies the maximum number of documents that may be buffered in the `IndexWriter` before they are written to the index. The only reason you might want to use this parameter is if you want more predictable behavior during indexing. That is, if you want the index to be committed every 100 documents, you could set `:max_buffered_docs` to 100. Otherwise, you are better off setting it to a `Ferret::FIX_INT_MAX` so that the number of buffered documents is limited only by the `:max_buffer_memory` limit.

:max_merged_docs

This parameter specifies the maximum number of documents allowed in any one segment. This is useful if your index is growing larger than 2 Gb. (Alternatively, you could rebuild Ferret with large-file support. If you can't work out how to do this, check Ferret's mailing list. There is bound to be someone there who will help you.) You can set `:max_merged_docs` to whatever value stops segments from being merged into a single segment that is greater than 2 Gb in size. For example, if the index goes over the file size limit at 1,000,000 documents, you can set `@:max_merged_docs` to 100,000. That way, when you get to 1,000,000 documents, instead of merging the ten 100,000-document segments, they will remain as they are. When you hit 2,000,000 documents, you'll have twenty 100,000-document segments. If you are working with indexes of this size, though, you should really build Ferret with large-file support.

:max_field_length

Sometimes, particularly when indexing data from the Web, you don't know how large the input documents are going to be. In this case, it is often a good idea to set a limit to the maximum length of the document that you want to index. Other times, you may want to index only the first 1,000 terms from a document, just to save disk space and/or improve performance. You can do this by setting the `:max_field_length` for the index. This parameter specifies the maximum number of terms that will be indexed from any one field.

By default, Ferret indexes the first 10,000 terms from each field. You can make Ferret index all terms from all fields by setting `:max_field_length` to `Ferret::FIX_INT_MAX`.

:use_compound_file

We already mentioned that one problem you may encounter is hitting your operating system's limit for the number of open file descriptors. Each segment has up to 10 files plus another file for every indexed field that doesn't omit norms.

> When a field's `omit_norms` property is set to `true`, a norms file is no longer needed for the field. See the "FieldInfo" section in Chapter 2.

If you start working with a large number of indexes, these numbers can add up. To prevent this problem, Ferret uses a compound file format by default, which basically writes all the files from a segment to a single file. This greatly reduces the number of file descriptors needed to read an index. However, it has a slightly degrading effect on the performance of both indexing and searching, so you may want to switch this feature off.

:index_skip_interval

This parameter allows you to control the structure of the term dictionary. The term dictionary is implemented as a skip list. (A good description of skip lists can be found on Wikipedia at *http://en.wikipedia.org/wiki/Skip_list*.)

This means that every *n*th term (where *n* is the index skip interval) is added to a term dictionary index. This index is loaded into memory in its entirety when the `IndexWriter` is opened and is used to quickly find search terms in the underlying disk-based term dictionary. As you may have already deduced, setting *n* to a smaller value will improve search speed at the cost of using more memory when the term dictionary index is loaded. As a result of having to write a larger term dictionary index to disk, indexing performance will also be a little slower. If you have enough memory, you might want to play around with different values for the index skip interval. However, it turns out that looking up terms in the term dictionary is not usually the bottleneck in searching, so you might not see much difference in search speed. The default value of 128 seems to be fine in most cases.

:doc_skip_interval

Within the term dictionary, the document lists are also implemented as skip lists. The same payoffs apply here as for `:index_skip_interval`. Think about the index at the end of a book. Each term in the index is followed by a list of pages that term appears on. Similarly, each term in the Ferret term dictionary references a list of documents that term appears in. Again, you can play around with this value, but don't expect too much. The default value of 16 will work fine in most cases.

Indexing parameter testing

Let's finish this section by testing the indexing parameters we've just covered. We'll do this by revisiting our indexing code from Chapter 1. See Example 3-1.

Example 3-1. index_tuner.rb

```
#!/usr/bin/env ruby
require 'rubygems'
require 'ferret'
require 'fileutils'
include Ferret
include Ferret::Index

def usage(message = nil)
  puts message if message
  puts "ruby #{File.basename(__FILE__)} <data dir> <index dir> " +
       "[-<index-param>=<val>]*"
  exit(1)
end

usage() if ARGV.size < 2
usage("Directory '#{ARGV[0]}' doesn't exist.") unless File.directory?(ARGV[0])
$data_dir = ARGV.shift
$index_dir = ARGV.shift
begin
  FileUtils.mkdir_p($index_dir)
rescue
  usage("Can't create index directory '#$index_dir'.")
end

options = {:path => $index_dir, :create => true}

# Add any options that were passed on the command line.
ARGV.each do |arg|
  if arg =~ /^-use_compound_file=(.+)$/
    value = $1.downcase
    options[:use_compound_file] = ["true", "t", "yes", "y"].include?(value)
  elsif arg =~ /^-(.+)=(.+)$/
    options[$1.to_sym] = $2.to_i
  else
    usage("Couldn't parse argument #{arg}")
  end
end

time = Time.now

index = Index.new(options)
Dir["#$data_dir/**/*.txt"].each do |file_name|
  index << {:file_name => file_name, :content => File.read(file_name)}
end
index.optimize()
index.close()
```

```
puts "Indexing finished in #{Time.now - time} seconds"
```

This script does exactly the same thing as the indexer we used in Chapter 1. The only difference is that it allows us to set the indexing parameters from the command line. Here is an example using the freely available Reuters-21578 (see *http://www.daviddlewis.com/resources/testcollections/reuters21578/*):

```
dave$ ruby index_tuner.rb corpus/ index/
Indexing finished in 29.728591 seconds
dave$ ruby index_tuner.rb corpus/ index/ -use_compound_file=false
Indexing finished in 24.28098 seconds
dave$ ruby index_tuner.rb corpus/ index/ -max_buffer_memory=268435456
Indexing finished in 22.449688 seconds
dave$ ruby index_tuner.rb corpus/ index/ -index_skip_interval=32 -doc_skip_interval=
Indexing finished in 32.540786 seconds
```

There is a lot of free data out there for you to test your indexer on, such as the Reuters-21578 collection. When tuning your indexer, though, it is important that you tune it on data similar to what you will be using in your application. For example, the perfect set of parameters for indexing all the books from Project Gutenberg won't necessarily be the best parameters for indexing a high-volume mailing list.

Parallel Indexing

So you've tuned Ferret to its absolute limit, but you still aren't getting the performance you need. The next possibility is parallel indexing. This involves setting up multiple separate indexing processes that each have their own index. Make sure that each index is created with exactly the same `FieldInfos` field setup. Once indexing is complete, you can merge all the indexes with the `IndexWriter#add_indexes` method, as shown in Example 3-2.

Example 3-2. Index merging

```
$: << File.dirname(__FILE__)
require 'assert'
require 'rubygems'
require 'ferret'

include Ferret::Index

5.times do |i|
  name = "index#{i}"
  i = Ferret::I.new(:path => "path/to/#{name}", :create => true)
  i << {:name => name}
  i.close
end

readers = []
readers << IndexReader.new("path/to/index0")
```

```
readers << IndexReader.new("path/to/index1")
readers << IndexReader.new("path/to/index2")
readers << IndexReader.new("path/to/index3")
readers << IndexReader.new("path/to/index4")

index_writer = IndexWriter.new(:path => "path/to/final/index")
index_writer.add_readers(readers)
index_writer.close()
readers.each {|reader| reader.close()}

i = Ferret::I.new(:path => 'path/to/final/index')
res = i.search('name*')
assert(res.hits.size, 5)
```

Optimizing the Index

You now know that the indexing process can leave any number of segments in the index. Although indexing performance is unaffected by the number of segments in the index, search performance does depend on the number of segments. The fewer segments, the better the search performance. When you open an index for reading, each segment is opened with its own `SegmentReader`. Each of those `SegmentReaders` has its own term dictionary, term enumerators, document enumerators, etc., so they can chew up quite a few resources, not to mention the fact that each reader needs to be searched separately. Therefore, the fewer the segments the better when searching the index. This is even more important when running short-lived command-line programs. It takes much more time to read in an unoptimized index than to read in an optimized index.

`IndexWriter` has an `optimize` method that minimizes the number of segments in an index, making the index optimal for searching. The best time to optimize the index is at the end of a batch indexing session. If, however, you are incrementally indexing your data—as you might do when indexing a model in a Rails application—you need to be more careful deciding when to optimize the index. The optimizing process itself can be quite resource-intensive, and it prevents any other documents from being added to the index. Thus, it is certainly not a good idea to optimize the index after each document is added to the index.

It should be noted that for large indexes, some processes—like sorting—can take a *very* long time on unoptimized indexes. Sometimes it takes a lot longer to sort an unoptimized index than to both optimize and sort the index. So, if you are having performance problems reading the index (searching, sorting, filtering, etc.), the first thing you should try is optimizing the index.

Index Locking and Concurrency Issues

This section deals with one of the most confusing issues for users new to Ferret: index locking. Ferret was designed to be used in a multiprocess environment, so it comes with a built-in index locking mechanism. Basically, you can't have two processes modifying the same index at the same time. And just because you are working in a single-process, single-threaded environment, it doesn't mean you can forget about index locking. Let's say, for example, that you want to delete a set of documents in the index by their document numbers, but you also have an `IndexWriter` open for adding documents to the index. You will need to close the `IndexWriter` before committing the deletions and then reopen the `IndexWriter`. Why, you ask? To answer this, you have to understand how index locking works.

The Ferret index currently uses two locks: a *commit lock* and a *write lock*. You must know which operations use which one of these locks and when. There are two classes that can obtain these locks: `IndexWriter` and `IndexReader`. The `IndexWriter` obtains the write lock as soon as it is opened and keeps it until it is closed. (Hence, the importance of closing `IndexWriter`s when you have finished with them.) As a result, you can only ever have one `IndexWriter` open on an index at any time, and you can't perform any write operations with an `IndexReader` while there is an `IndexWriter` open on the index. `IndexWriter` will also obtain the commit lock when you optimize, commit, or close the index. Furthermore, `IndexWriter` will obtain the commit lock unpredictably during indexing. `IndexWriter` will commit the index whenever segments are merged, so it is difficult to predict exactly when it will obtain the commit lock, except to say that it may happen whenever a document is added to the index.

`IndexReader`, on the other hand, acquires the write lock only when a write operation is called. There are three of these: `delete`, `undelete`, and `set_norm`. The commit lock is acquired only when you call the `IndexReader`'s `commit` method, and then only if the `IndexReader` has any modifications. This becomes clearer if you consider `IndexReader` to have two separate roles. One is a read-only class that is used as the interface to an `IndexSearcher`. The other is an index modifier used to modify documents (`delete` or `set_norm`) based on their document IDs.

You can have as many `IndexReader`s open on an index as you like, even if there is an `IndexWriter` open on the index. You can, therefore, happily run multiple concurrent searches on the index at the same time. What you can't do is have multiple index modifying classes open at the same time. Avoid using `IndexReader`'s `delete` method in favor of `IndexWriter`'s `delete` method.

Multithreaded Environment

Ferret works well in a multithreaded environment. `IndexWriter`, `IndexReader`, and even the `Index` class are all thread-safe, so they can be shared by multiple threads. In fact, the `IndexWriter` needs to be shared by all threads, as you can't have more than one `IndexWriter` open on an index at one time. Again, avoid using `IndexReader`'s `delete` method. If you have to use it, you will run into the same issues as in a single-threaded environment—you have to close the `IndexWriter` whenever you want call `delete`, `undelete`, or `set_norm` on an `IndexReader`.

As far as searching goes, it is up to you whether you want each thread to have its own `IndexReader` or to share one `IndexReader` between threads. It is hard to say which would perform better, although multiple `IndexReaders` will certainly use much more memory. `IndexReaders` use a lot of memory to make index access as fast as possible, so if memory is an issue, you should avoid opening multiple `IndexReaders`.

Multiprocess Environment

As most people seem to be using Ferret in Rails applications, we commonly see Ferret working in a multiprocess environment. The key to running Ferret successfully in a multiprocess environment is, as always, to make sure you have only one object modifying the index at any one time. This leaves you with a few options. If you can, try to restrict index modification to a single process. All the other processes can be used for searching.

If all of the processes must modify the indexed data, then you will need a different solution. One way to go about it is to have each process open the `IndexWriter` only for the time it needs to modify the index. The `Index` class can do this if you set the `:auto_flush` parameter to `true`. This is a very simple solution but it is not very high performing.

Another solution is to mark the rows in the database as they are modified. You can then use a separate batch indexing process to go through the database and update the index. This solution will give the best performance as far as indexing goes, but there will be a lag between the time the data is modified and the time it appears in search results.

Finally, you can implement a Ferret index server. This shouldn't be too difficult using DRb (Distributed Ruby).

Summary

In this chapter, we covered some advanced indexing topics. You learned a little about what happens behind the scenes during the indexing process. We covered performance tuning for both indexing and searching in some detail, and we explained the Ferret index locking mechanism, briefly touching on some concurrency issues. By this stage, you are probably chomping at the bit to find out how to search the indexes you've been building. We will cover that in Chapter 4.

CHAPTER 4

Search

Everything you've learned so far about creating indexes is pretty useless if you don't know how to use those indexes to find what you are looking for. After all, that's what Ferret is for. This chapter covers everything you need to know about searching in Ferret. We'll start with the basic search classes followed by the various types of query. We'll then talk about the query parser and Ferret's own query language—FQL. We'll then cover some more advanced topics such as sorting, filtering, and highlighting.

Overview of Searching Classes

Ferret's search API is about as simple as its indexing API. In fact, if you are using the `Index` class, all you have to know is the `search_each()` method and a little bit of Ferret's query language and you are set. However, if you take the time to learn the rest of the search API, you'll discover a wealth of opportunities you didn't even know existed.

The search API consists of the following classes:

- `IndexSearcher`
- `Query`
- `QueryParser`
- `Filter`
- `Sort`

IndexSearcher

`IndexSearcher`, as the name would suggest, is used to search indexes. You can also use it to highlight and explain query results and read documents from the index (as you would with `IndexReader`). To create an `IndexSearcher`, you need to supply it with an `IndexReader`:

```
reader = IndexReader.new("path/to/index")
searcher = Searcher.new(reader)
```

As usual, you can shortcut this by supplying it with a `Directory` or a filesystem path to the index:

```
searcher = Searcher.new("path/to/index")
```

Ferret's MultiSearcher Class

Ferret also offers a `MultiSearcher`; however, its use is not recommended because you can do everything the `MultiSearcher` can do with an `IndexSearcher` by supplying it with a `MultiReader`:

```
readers = []
readers << IndexReader.new("path/to/index1")
readers << IndexReader.new("path/to/index2")
readers << IndexReader.new("path/to/index3")
multi_reader = IndexReader.new(readers)
searcher = Searcher.new(multi-reader)
```

Query

Ferret contains more than 15 different types of query, each of which you'll learn about later in this chapter. Basically, queries are built and combined to specify what exactly it is you are looking for. You can then pass them to the `IndexSearcher` so it will retrieve your result set. Queries are the fundamental building block of the search API.

QueryParser

With more than 15 different types of query (each with its own definitive API), it can get quite tedious to build them by hand. Succinct as Ruby code is, it is much easier to build queries using a simple query language, not to mention the fact that you wouldn't want users to have to type Ruby code into your search box. For example, let's say we wanted to search for all articles in a blog that have the words "ruby" and "ferret" in either the title field or the content field. You could use the `QueryParser`:

```
query = query_parser.parse("title|content:(ruby AND ferret)")
```

Or you could build the query yourself. The `QueryParser` is the magic behind the `Index` class that makes it so easy to use.

Filter

You can already specify exactly which documents you want to find using the various `Query` classes, so you might be wondering what you need a `Filter` class for. `Filters` have a few purposes. First, `Filters` actually cache their results, so if you have a particular query that is run over and over again, you might want to convert it to a `Filter` to improve performance. Second, `Filters` can be used to apply common constraints to `Queries`. For example, to restrict a user's search to only published articles, you would use a `Filter`. Or you might let users filter their own searches with a drop-down menu of common filters, perhaps a filter that restricts search results to the last month or the last seven days. This is particularly useful because most users won't know the range query syntax. You'll learn more about when to use a filter and how to create your own filter later in this chapter.

Sort

By default, the `IndexSearcher` returns your query results in order of relevance. If you want to sort the results in any other way, you are going to have to use the `Sort` class. As discussed earlier in Chapter 2, you can currently sort by `Integer`, `Float`, and `String`. We'll cover this in more detail in the "Sorting Search Results" section later in this chapter.

Building Queries

Even if you are using the `QueryParser` to build all your queries, you'll gain a better understanding of how searching works in Ferret by building each of the queries by hand. We'll also include the Ferret Query Language (FQL) syntax for each different type of query as we go. As you read, you'll find some queries that you can't build even using the `QueryParser`, so it will be useful to learn about them as well.

Before we get started, we should mention that each `Query` has a boost field. Because you will usually be combining queries with a `BooleanQuery`, it can be useful to give some of those queries a higher weighting than the other clauses in the `BooleanQuery`. All `Query` objects also implement `hash` and `eql?`, so they can be used in a `HashTable` to cache query results.

Tokenizing Query Terms

When building queries by hand, it is important to consider how the data is tokenized when you add terms to the queries. For example, "red-face" could be stored in the index as a single term or it might be stored as two terms, "red" and "face". You need to make sure that you build queries with this in mind.

If "red-face" is tokenized as a single term, you can use a `TermQuery`. If it's tokenized as two separate terms, you'll need to use a `PhraseQuery`.

It becomes more complicated when you use an analyzer that stems and removes stop words. If you try to use a `TermQuery` to search for the word "the" when your analyzer removed stop words, you'll likely get no results. If you used a stemmer, you need to make sure you also stem the terms you are using in your queries. And lastly—this is a very common mistake—make sure you downcase your terms if that's what your analyzer did. This is another very common gotcha for new Ferret users. `QueryParser` handles all of that for you. You just need to make sure it uses the same analyzer that you used to analyze the data during indexing.

TermQuery

`TermQuery` is the most basic of all queries and is actually the building block for most of the other queries (even where you wouldn't expect it, like in `WildcardQuery` and `FuzzyQuery`). It is very simple to use. All you need to do is specify the field you want to search in and the term you want to search for:

```
# FQL: "title:shawshank"
query = TermQuery.new(:title, "shawshank")
```

BooleanQuery

`BooleanQueries` are used to combine other queries. Combined with `TermQuery`, they cover most of the queries users use every day on the major search engines. We already saw an example of a `BooleanQuery` earlier, but we didn't explain how it works. A `BooleanQuery` is implemented as a list of `BooleanClauses`. Each clause has a type: `:should`, `:must`, or `:must_not`. `:should` clauses add value to the relevance score when they are found, but the query won't reject a document just because the clause isn't present. This is the type of clause you would find in an "or" query. A `:must` clause, on the other hand, *must* be present in a document for that document to be returned as a hit. Finally, a `:must_not` clause causes the `BooleanQuery` to reject all documents that contain that clause. For example, say we want to find all documents that contain the word "rails", but we don't want the documents about trains, and we'd especially like the "rails" documents that all contain the term "ruby". We'd implement this query like this:

```
# FQL: "content:(+rails -train ruby)"
query = BooleanQuery.new()
query.add_query(TermQuery.new(:content, "rails"), :must)
query.add_query(TermQuery.new(:content, "train"), :must_not)
query.add_query(TermQuery.new(:content, "ruby"),  :should)
```

One rule to remember when creating `BooleanQueries` is that every `BooleanQuery` must include at least one `:must` or `:should` parameter. A `BooleanQuery` with only `:must_not` clauses will not raise any exceptions, but it also won't return any results. If you want to find all documents without a certain attribute, you should add a `MatchAllQuery` to your `BooleanQuery`. Let's say you want to find all documents without the word "spam":

```
# FQL: "* -content:spam"
query = BooleanQuery.new()
query.add_query(MatchAllQuery.new, :should)
query.add_query(TermQuery.new(:content, "spam"), :must_not)
```

PhraseQuery

Once you add `PhraseQuery` to your bag of tricks, you can build pretty much any query that most users would apply in their daily search engine usage. You build queries by adding one term at a time with a position increment. For example, let's say that we want to search for the phrase "quick brown fox". We'd build the query like this:

```
# FQL: 'content:"quick brown fox"'
query = PhraseQuery.new(:content)
query.add_term("quick", 1)
query.add_term("brown", 1)
query.add_term("fox", 1)
```

Ferret's `PhraseQueries` offer a little more than usual phrase queries. You can actually skip positions in the phrase. For example, let's say we don't care what color the fox is; we just want a "quick <> fox". We can implement this query like this:

```
# FQL: 'content:"quick <> fox"'
query = PhraseQuery.new(:content)
query.add_term("quick", 1)
query.add_term("fox", 2)
```

What if we want a "red", "brown", or "pink" fox that is either "fast" or "quick"? We can actually add multiple terms to a position at a time:

```
# FQL: 'content:"quick|fast red|brown|pink fox"'
query = PhraseQuery.new(:content)
query.add_term(["quick", "fast"], 1)
query.add_term(["red", "brown", "pink"], 1)
query.add_term("fox", 1)
```

So far, we've been strict with the order and positions of the terms. But Ferret also allows *sloppy* phrases. That means the phrase doesn't need to be exact; it just needs to be close enough. Let's say you want to find all documents mentioning "red-faced politicians". You'd also want all documents containing the

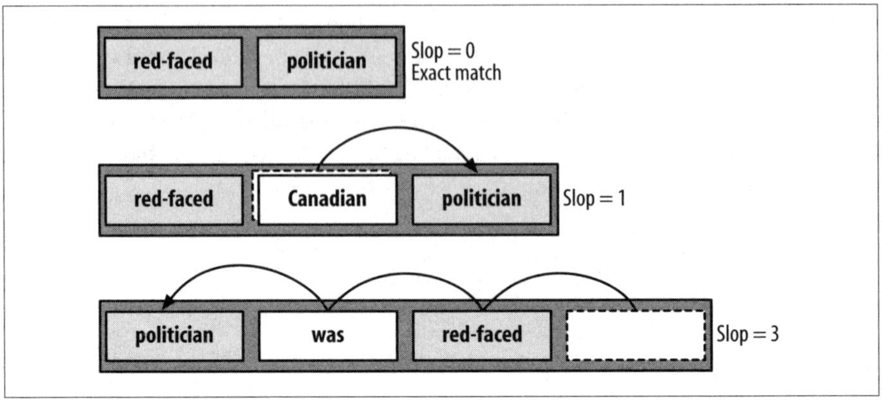

Figure 4-1. Sloppy PhraseQuery

phrase "red-faced Canadian politician" or even "the politician was red-faced". This is where sloppy queries come in handy:

```
# FQL: 'content:"red-faced politician"~4'
query = PhraseQuery.new(:content, 4) # set the slop to 4
query.add_term("red-faced", 1)
query.add_term("politician", 1)

# you can also change the slop like this
query.slop = 1
```

The key to understanding sloppy phrase queries is knowing how the slop is calculated. You can think of a phrase's "slop" as its "edit distance". It is the minimum number of steps that you need to move the terms from the original search phrase to get the phrase occurring in the document (see Figure 4-1).

The first phrase is an exact match, so the slop is 0. In the next phrase you need to move "politician" right once, so the slop is 1. The third phrase shows that the terms don't need to be in order. Just move "politician" left three times and you have a match. Hence, the slop is 3.

Sloppy Phrase Queries As Boolean Queries

The standard `BooleanQuery` in Ferret doesn't take into account the distance between matching terms. In some cases, this can give you inaccurate results. For example, if you want to search for "ferret" and "rails", you could use the `BooleanQuery`. But your result set might include documents talking about "rails" at the beginning and "ferret" at the end of the document and nothing about the two together. To solve this problem, you could use a `PhraseQuery` with a relatively large slop. This will match documents with the two terms relatively close together and will actually give a higher score the closer together the terms are:

```
# FQL: 'content:"ferret&rails"~200'
query = PhraseQuery.new(:content, 200) # set the slop to 200
query.add_term("ferret", 0)
query.add_term("rails", 0)
```

RangeQuery

Now we are getting into some of the more specialized queries available in Ferret. RangeQuery does exactly what you would expect it to do: it searches for ranges of values. Most of the time, RangeQueries are used on date or number fields. Make sure you have these set up correctly as described in the "Date Fields" section in Chapter 2. For example, if you want to search for all blog entries between June 1, 2005 and March 15, 2006, you could build the query like this:

```
# FQL: 'date:[20050501 20060315]'
query = RangeQuery.new(:date, :lower => "20050501", :upper => "20060315")
```

We don't need to include both ends of the range. We could search for all entries before Christmas 2005:

```
# FQL: 'date:<20051225]'
query = RangeQuery.new(:date, :upper => "20051225")
```

Or all entries after Christmas 2005:

```
# FQL: 'date:[20051225>'
query = RangeQuery.new(:date, :lower => "20051225")
```

So, what happens to the blog entries from Christmas day in these two examples? Both queries return blog entries from Christmas day because these bounds are inclusive. That is, they include all terms where :lower <= term <= :upper. We can easily make RangeQuery bounds exclusive. If we want to make the first example exclusive, we write it like this:

```
# FQL: 'date:{20050501 20060315}'
query = RangeQuery.new(:date,
                       :lower_exclusive => "20050501",
                       :upper_exclusive => "20060315")
```

This feature is useful for paging through documents by field value. Say we want to page through all the products in our database by price, starting with all products under $10, then all products between $10 and $20, etc., up to $100. We could do it like this:

```
10.times do |i|
  lower_price = "%06.2f" % (i * 10)
  upper_price = "%06.2f" % ((i + 1) * 10)

  query = RangeQuery.new(:price,
                         :lower => lower_price,
```

```
                            :upper_exclusive => upper_price)

    puts "products from $#{lower_price.to_f} to $#{upper_price.to_f}"
    index.search_each(query) do |doc_id, score|
      puts "    #{index[doc_id][:title]}"
    end
  end
```

RangeQuery will work just as well on string fields. Just keep in mind that the terms are always sorted as if they were binary strings, so you may get some unexpected results if you are sorting multibyte character encodings.

MultiTermQuery

This is kind of like an optimized Boolean OR query. The optimization comes from the fact that it searches only a single field, making lookup a lot faster because all clauses use the same section of the index. As usual, it is very simple to use. Let's say you want to find all documents with the term "fast" or a synonym for it:

```
# FQL: 'content:"fast|quick|rapid|speedy|swift"'
query = MultiTermQuery.new(:content)
query.add_term("quick")
query.add_term("fast")
query.add_term("speedy")
query.add_term("swift")
query.add_term("rapid")
```

But there's more. What if you would prefer documents with the term "quick" and you don't really like the term "speedy"? You can program it like this:

```
# FQL: 'content:"speedy^0.5|fast|rapid|swift|quick^10.0"'
query = MultiTermQuery.new(:content)
query.add_term("quick", 10.0)
query.add_term("fast")
query.add_term("speedy", 0.5)
query.add_term("swift")
query.add_term("rapid")
```

You may be wondering what use this is, since we can perform this query (including the term weighting) with a BooleanQuery. The reason it is included is that it is used internally by a few of the more advanced queries that we'll be looking at in a moment: PrefixQuery, WildcardQuery, and FuzzyQuery. In Apache Lucene, these queries are rewritten as BooleanQueries and they tend to be very resource-expensive queries. But a BooleanQuery for this task is overkill, and there are a few optimizations we can make because we know all terms are in the same field and all clauses are :should clauses. For this reason, MultiTermQuery was created, making WildcardQuery and FuzzyQuery much more viable in Ferret.

When some of these queries are rewritten to `MultiTermQueries`, there is a risk that they will add too many terms to the query. Say someone comes along and submits the `WildcardQuery` "?*" (i.e., search for all terms). If you have a million terms in your index, you could run into some memory overflow problems. To prevent this, `MultiTermQuery` has a `:max_terms` limit that is set to 512 by default. You can set this to whatever value you like. If you try to add too many terms, by default the lowest scored terms will be dropped without any warnings. You can increase the `:max_terms` like this:

```
query = MultiTermQuery.new(:content, :max_terms => 1024)
```

You also have the option of setting a minimum score. This is another way to limit the number of terms added to the query. It is used by `FuzzyQuery`, in which case the range of scores is `0..1.0`. You shouldn't use this parameter in either `PrefixQuery` or `WildcardQuery`. The only other time you would probably use this is when building a custom query of your own:

```
query = MultiTermQuery.new(:content,
                           :max_terms => 1024,
                           :min_score => 0.5)
```

PrefixQuery

The `PrefixQuery` is useful if you want to store a hierarchy of categories in the index as you might do for blog entries. You could store them using a Unix filename-like string:

```
index << { :category => "/sport/"                }
index << { :category => "/sport/judo/"           }
index << { :category => "/sport/swimming/"       }
index << { :category => "/coding/"               }
index << { :category => "/coding/c/"             }
index << { :category => "/coding/c/ferret"       }
index << { :category => "/coding/lisp/"          }
index << { :category => "/coding/ruby/"          }
index << { :category => "/coding/ruby/ferret/"   }
index << { :category => "/coding/ruby/hpricot/"  }
index << { :category => "/coding/ruby/mongrel/"  }
```

Note that the `:category` field in this case should be untokenized. Now you can find all entries relating to Ruby using a `PrefixQuery`:

```
# FQL: 'category:/coding/ruby/*'
query = PrefixQuery.new(:category, "/coding/ruby/")
```

`PrefixQuery` is the first of the queries covered here that use the `MultiTermQuery`. As we mentioned in the previous section, `MultiTermQuery` has a maximum number of terms that can be inserted. Let's say you have 2,000 categories and someone submits the prefix query with `/` as the prefix, the root category. Ferret will try to load all 2,000 categories into the `MultiTermQuery`, but MultiTermQuery will only allow the first 512 and no more—all others will be ignored. You can change this behavior when you create the PrefixQuery using the :max_terms property:

```
# FQL: 'category:/*'
query = PrefixQuery.new(:category, "/",
                        :max_terms => 1024)
```

WildcardQuery

WildcardQuery allows you to run searches with two simple wildcards: * matches any number of characters (0..infinite), and ? matches a single character. If you look at PrefixQuery's FQL, you'll notice that it looks like a WildcardQuery. Actually, if you build a WildcardQuery with only a single * at the end of the term and no ?, it will be rewritten internally, during search, to a PrefixQuery. Add to that, if you create a WildcardQuery with no wildcards, it will be rewritten internally to a TermQuery. The Wildcard API is pretty similar to PrefixQuery:

```
# FQL: 'content:dav?d*'
query = WildcardQuery.new(:content, "dav?d*")
```

Just like PrefixQuery, WildcardQuery uses MultiTermQuery internally, so you can also set the :max_terms property:

```
# FQL: 'content:f*'
query = WildcardQuery.new(:content, "f*",
                          :max_terms => 1024)
```

You should be very careful with WildcardQueries. Any query that begins with a wildcard character (* or ?) will cause the searcher to enumerate and scan the entire field's term index. This can be quite a performance hit for a very large index. You might want to reject any WildcardQueries that don't have a non-wildcard prefix.

There is one gotcha we should mention here. Say you want to select all the documents that have a :price field. You might first try:

```
# FQL: 'price:*'
query = WildcardQuery.new(:price, "*")
```

This looks like it should work, right? The problem is, * matches even empty fields and actually gets optimized into a MatchAllQuery. On the bright side, the performance problems that plague WildcardQueries that start with a wildcard character don't actually apply to plain old * searches. So, back to the problem at hand, we can find all documents with a :price field like this:

```
# FQL: 'price:?*'
query = WildcardQuery.new(:price, "?*")
```

However, don't forget about the performance implications of doing this. Think about building a custom `Filter` to perform this operation instead.

FuzzyQuery

`FuzzyQuery` is to `TermQuery` what a sloppy `PhraseQuery` is to an exact `PhraseQuery`. `FuzzyQueries` match terms that are close to each other but not exact. For example, "color" is very close to "colour". `FuzzyQuery` can be used to match both of these terms. Not only that, but they are great for matching misspellings like "collor" or "colro". We can build the query like this:

```
# FQL: 'content:color~'
query = FuzzyQuery.new(:content, "color")
```

Again, just like `PrefixQuery`, `FuzzyQuery` uses `MultiTermQuery` internally so you can also set the `:max_terms` property:

```
# FQL: 'content:color~'
query = FuzzyQuery.new(:content, "color",
                       :max_terms => 1024)
```

`FuzzyQuery` is implemented using the Levenshtein distance algorithm (*http://en.wikipedia.org/wiki/Levenshtein_distance*). The Levenshtein distance is similar to slop. It is the number of edits needed to convert one term to another. So "color" and "colour" have a Levenshtein distance score of 1.0 because a single letter has been added. "Colour" and "coller" have a Levenshtein distance score of 2.0 because two letters have been replaced. A match is determined by calculating the score for a match. This is calculated with the following formula, where *target* is the term we want to match and *term* is the term we are matching in the index.

Levenshtein distance score:

```
1 - distance / min(target.size, term.size)
```

This means that an exact match will have a score of 1.0, whereas terms with no corresponding letters will have a score of 0.0. Since `FuzzyQuery` has a limit to the number of matching terms it can use, the lowest scoring matches get discarded if the `FuzzyQuery` becomes full.

Because of the way `FuzzyQuery` is implemented, it needs to scan every single term in its field's index to find all valid similar terms in the dictionary. This can take a long time if you have a large index. One way to prevent any performance problems is to set a minimum prefix length. Do this by setting the `:min_prefix_len` parameter when creating the `FuzzyQuery`. This parameter is set to 0 by default; hence, the fact that it would need to scan every term in index.

To minimize the expense of finding matching terms, we could set the minimum prefix length of the example query to 3. This would greatly reduce the number of terms that need to be enumerated, and "color" would still match "colour", although "cloor" would no longer match:

```
# FQL: 'content:color~' => no way to set :min_prefix_length in FQL
query = FuzzyQuery.new(:content, "color",
                       :max_terms => 1024,
                       :min_prefix_length => 3)
```

You can also set a cut-off score for matching terms by setting the `:min_similarity` parameter. This will not affect how many terms are enumerated, but it will affect how many terms are added to the internal `MultiTermQuery`, which can also help improve performance:

```
# FQL: 'content:color~0.8' => no way to set :min_prefix_length in FQL
query = FuzzyQuery.new(:content, "color",
                       :max_terms => 1024,
                       :min_similarity => 0.8,
                       :min_prefix_length => 3)
```

In some cases, you may want to change the default values for `:min_prefix_len` and `:min_similarity`, particularly for use in the Ferret `QueryParser`. Simply set the class variables in `FuzzyQuery`:

```
FuzzyQuery.default_min_similarity = 0.8
FuzzyQuery.default_prefix_length = 3
```

MatchAllQuery

This query matches all documents in the index. The only time you'd really want to use this is in combination with a negative clause in a `BooleanQuery` or in combination with a filter, although `ConstantScoreQuery` makes more sense for the latter:

```
# FQL: '* -content:spam'
query = BooleanQuery.new()
query.add_query(MatchAllQuery.new, :should)
query.add_query(TermQuery.new(:content, "spam"), :must_not)
```

ConstantScoreQuery

This query is kind of like `MatchAllQuery` except that it is combined with a `Filter`. This is useful when you need to apply more than one filter to a query. It is also used internally by `RangeQuery`. "Constant Score" means that all hits returned by this query have the same score, which makes sense for queries like `RangeQueries` where either a document is in the range or it isn't:

```
# FQL: 'date:[20050501 20060315]'
filter = RangeFilter.new(:date, :lower => "20050501", :upper => "20060315")
query = ConstantScoreQuery.new(filter)
```

FilteredQuery

So, what is the difference between this query and the previous one? Not a lot, really. The following two queries are equivalent:

```
# FQL: 'date:[20050501 20060315] && content:ruby'
query1 = FilteredQuery.new(TermQuery.new(:content, "ruby"),
                           RangeFilter.new(:date,
                                           :lower => "20050501",
                                           :upper => "20060315"))

# FQL: 'date:[20050501 20060315] && content:ruby'
filter = RangeFilter.new(:date, :lower => "20050501", :upper => "20060315")
query2 = BooleanQuery.new()
query2.add_query(TermQuery.new(:content, "ruby"), :must)
query2.add_query(ConstantScoreQuery.new(filter), :must)
```

It's really just a matter of taste. There is a slight performance advantage to using a `FilteredQuery`, although the `QueryParser` will create a `BooleanQuery`.

Span Queries

Span queries are a little different from the queries we've covered so far in that they take into account the range of the terms matched. In the "PhraseQuery" section earlier in this chapter, we talked about using `PhraseQuery` to implement a simple Boolean `AND` query that ensured that the terms were close together. Span queries are designed to do that and more.

A couple of things to note here. First, span queries can contain only other span queries, although they can be combined with other queries using a `BooleanQuery`. Second, any one span query can contain only a single field. Even when you are using `SpanOrQuery`, you must ensure that all span queries added are on the same field; otherwise, an `ArgumentError` will be raised.

SpanTermQuery

The `SpanTermQuery` is the basic building block for span queries. It's almost identical to the basic `TermQuery`. The difference is that it enumerates the positions of its matches. These positions are used by the rest of the span queries:

```
include Ferret::Search::Spans
# FQL: There is no Ferret Query Language for SpanQueries yet
query = SpanTermQuery.new(:content, "ferret")
```

Because of the position enumeration, `SpanTermQuery` will be slower than a plain `TermQuery`, so it should be used only in combination with other span queries.

SpanFirstQuery

This is where span queries start to get interesting. `SpanFirstQuery` matches terms within a limited distance from the start of the field, the distance being a parameter to the constructor. This type of query can be useful because often the terms occurring at the start of a document are the most important terms in a document. To find all documents with "ferret" within the first 100 terms of the `:content` field, we do this:

```
include Ferret::Search::Spans
# FQL: There is no Ferret Query Language for SpanQueries yet
query = SpanTermQuery.new(:content, "ferret")
```

SpanOrQuery

This query is pretty easy to understand. It is just like a `BooleanQuery` that does only `:should` clauses. With this query we can find all documents with the term "rails" in the first 100 terms of the `:content` field and the term "ferret" anywhere:

```
# FQL: There is no Ferret Query Language for SpanQueries yet
span_term_query = SpanTermQuery.new(:content, "rails")
span_first_query = SpanFirstQuery.new(span_term_query, 100)
span_term_query = SpanTermQuery.new(:content, "ferret")

query = SpanOrQuery.new()
query.add(span_term_query)
query.add(span_first_query)
```

Let's reiterate here that all span queries you add to `SpanOrQuery` must be on the same field.

SpanNotQuery

This query can be used to exclude span queries. This gives us the ability to exclude documents based on span queries, as you would do with a `:must_not` clause in a `BooleanQuery`. Let's exclude all documents matched by the previous query that contain the terms "otter" or "train":

```
# FQL: There is no Ferret Query Language for SpanQueries yet
span_term_query = SpanTermQuery.new(:content, "rails")
span_first_query = SpanFirstQuery.new(span_term_query, 100)

inclusive_query = SpanOrQuery.new()
inclusive_query.add(span_first_query)
inclusive_query.add(SpanTermQuery.new(:content, "ferret"))
```

```
exclusive_query = SpanOrQuery.new()
exclusive_query.add(SpanTermQuery.new(:content, "otter"))
exclusive_query.add(SpanTermQuery.new(:content, "train"))

query = SpanNotQuery.new(inclusive_query, exclusive_query)
```

SpanNearQuery

This is the one you've been waiting for, the king of all span queries. This allows you to specify a range for all the queries it contains. For example, if we set the range to equal 100, all span queries within this query must have matches within 100 terms of each other or the document won't be a match. Let's simply search for all documents with the terms "ferret", "ruby", and "rails" within a 50 term range:

```
# FQL: There is no Ferret Query Language for SpanQueries yet
query = SpanNearQuery.new(:slop => 50)
query.add(SpanTermQuery.new(:content, "ferret"))
query.add(SpanTermQuery.new(:content, "ruby"))
query.add(SpanTermQuery.new(:content, "rails"))
```

Actually, we could have just done that with a sloppy `PhraseQuery`. But by combining other span queries, we can do a lot of things that a sloppy `PhraseQuery` can't handle. One other thing that a sloppy `PhraseQuery` can't do is force the terms to be in correct order. With the `SpanNearQuery`, we can force the terms to be in correct order:

```
# FQL: There is no Ferret Query Language for SpanQueries yet
query = SpanNearQuery.new(:slop => 50, :in_order => true) #set in_order to true
query.add(SpanTermQuery.new(:content, "ferret"))
query.add(SpanTermQuery.new(:content, "ruby"))
query.add(SpanTermQuery.new(:content, "rails"))
```

This will match only documents that have the terms "ferret", "ruby", and "rails" within 50 terms of each other and in that particular order.

Boosting Queries

We mentioned at the start of this chapter that you can boost queries. This can be very handy when you want to make one term more important than your other search terms. For example, let's say you want to search for all documents with the term "ferret" and the terms "ruby" or "rails", but you'd much rather have documents with "rails" than just "ruby". You'd implement the query like this:

```
# FQL: 'content:(+ferret rails^10.0 ruby^0.1))'
query = BooleanQuery.new()

term_query = TermQuery.new(:content, "ferret")
query.add_query(term_query, :must)
```

```
term_query = TermQuery.new(:content, "rails")
term_query.boost = 10.0
query.add_query(term_query, :should)

term_query = TermQuery.new(:content, "ruby")
term_query.boost = 0.1
query.add_query(term_query, :should)
```

Unlike boosts used in `Documents` and `Fields`, these boosts aren't translated to and from bytes so they don't lose any of their precision. As for deciding which values to use, it will still require a lot of experimentation. Use the `Search::Searcher#explain` and `Index::Index#explain` methods to see how different boost values affect scoring.

QueryParser

You've now been introduced to all the different types of queries available in Ferret, and you've learned how to build different queries by hand. Some of it probably seems like a lot of work and it's certainly not something you'd ask a user to do. Luckily, we can leave most of the work to the Ferret `QueryParser`. You've already seen many examples of the Ferret Query Language (FQL) in the previous section ("Building Queries"), and you'll have noticed that most of the queries you can build in code can be described much more easily in FQL. In this section, we'll talk about setting up the `QueryParser`, and then we'll go into more detail about FQL.

Setting Up the QueryParser

The `QueryParser` has a number of parameters, as shown in Table 4-1.

Table 4-1. QueryParser parameters

Parameter	Default	Short description
`:default_field`	`:*`	The default field to be searched; it can also be an array.
`:analyzer`	`StandardAnalyzer`	Analyzer used by the query parser to parse query terms.
`:wild_card_downcase`	`true`	Specifies whether wildcard queries should be downcased or not, since they are not analyzed by the parser.
`:fields`	`[]`	Lets the query parser know what fields are available for searching, particularly when the `:*` is specified as the search field.

Parameter	Default	Short description
:validate_fields	false	Set to true if you want an exception to be raised if there is an attempt to search a nonexistent field.
:or_default	true	Use OR as the default Boolean operator.
:default_slop	0	Default slop to use in PhraseQueries.
:handle_parser_errors	true	QueryParser will quietly handle all parsing errors internally. If you'd like to handle them yourself, set this parameter to false.
:clean_string	true	QueryParser will quickly review the query string to make sure that quotes and brackets match up and special characters are escaped.
:max_clauses	512	The maximum number of clauses allowed in Boolean queries and the maximum number of terms allowed in multi, prefix, wildcard, or fuzzy queries.

The first thing you need to think about when setting up the QueryParser is which analyzer to use. Preferably, you should use the same analyzer you used to tokenize your documents during indexing. This analyzer will be used to analyze all terms before they are added to queries, except in the case of wildcard queries, since they'll contain * and ?, which many analyzers won't accept. Because of this, you'll probably need to lowercase the wildcard query if the analyzer you used was a lowercasing analyzer. The exception to this rule is the use of wildcard queries on fields that are untokenized, in which case you might want to leave them as case-sensitive. To specify whether or not wildcard queries are lowercased, you need to set the parameter :wild_card_downcase. It is set to true by default.

The next thing you need to worry about is document fields. First of all, which fields are available to be searched? When the user specifies the field he wants to search, he can use an * to search all fields. For this to work, you need to set up the QueryParser so that it knows which fields are available. Simply set the parameter :fields to an array of field names. You can get the list of available field names from an IndexReader:

```
query = QueryParser.new(:fields => reader.fields,
                        :tokenized_fields => reader.tokenized_fields)
```

The :fields parameter can be either a Symbol or an Array of Symbols. You can also set the QueryParser to validate all queries that use these fields. That is, each time a user selects a field to search, the query parser will check that that field is present in the @fields attribute, and if it isn't, it will raise an exception. So, if your index has a :title and a :content field and the user tries to search in a :contetn field (note the misspelling), the QueryParser will raise an exception. To make the QueryParser validate fields, you need to set the :validate_fields parameter to true. It is set to false by default.

Once you have specified which fields are available, you need to designate which of those fields you want to be searched by default. Simply set the parameter :default_field to a single field name or an array of field names. You can even set it to the symbol :*, which will specify that you want to search all fields by default. :* is in fact the default value.

Next, you must decide if you want Boolean queries to be OR or AND by default. This involves setting :or_default to true or false. By default, it is set to true, but if you want to make your search more like a regular search engine, you should set it to false.

The QueryParser handles parse errors for you by default. It does this by trying to parse the query according to the grammar. If that fails, it tries to parse it into a simple term or Boolean query, ignoring all query language tokens. If it still can't do that, it will return an empty Boolean query. No exception will be thrown and the user will just see an empty set of results. If you'd like to handle the parse errors yourself, you can set the parameter :handle_parse_errors to false. You can then let the user know that the query she entered was invalid.

Also, to make QueryParser more robust, it has a clean_string method that basically makes sure brackets and quotes match up and that all special characters within phrase strings are properly escaped. For example, the following query:

```
(city:Braidwood AND shop:(Torpy's OR "Pig & Whistle
```

will be cleaned up as:

```
(city:Braidwood AND shop:(Torpy's OR "Pig \& Whistle"))
```

Perhaps you want to clean the query strings yourself or you would prefer to have an exception raised if the query can't be parsed. To do this, set the :clean_string parameter to false.

Because MultiTermQueries have a :max_terms property, you can set the default value used for :max_terms by the query parser by setting its :max_clauses parameter. This will also affect the maximum number of clauses you can add to a BooleanQuery.

Ferret Query Language

The Ferret Query Language allows you to build most of the queries that you can build with Ruby code using just a simple query string. For simple queries, it matches what users have come to expect from years of using different search engines. But FQL allows you to build much more diverse queries than the usual search engine queries allow. FQL aims to be as concise as possible while still being readable and hopefully obvious to most users.

Query String Tokenization

Before we get into specific query types, we should first look at the way query strings are parsed. The following characters have special meaning in `QueryParser`:

```
\ & : ( ) [ ] { } ! " ~ ^ | < > = * ? + -
```

Each of these characters, as well as whitespace, can be escaped with a backslash (\) to include it in a search term. Search terms are strings of characters separated by whitespace or by one of the special characters. Each search term will be further processed by the `QueryParser`'s analyzer, as described earlier in this chapter (unless it contains unescaped wildcard characters, such as * or ?). Here is an example of how a query string gets tokenized:

```
'title:Shawshank\ Redeption +date:<20000604 +topic:(jail friendship)'

=> [
     'title', ':', 'Shawshank Redeption', '+', 'date', ':', '<',
     '20000604', '+', 'topic', ':', '(', 'jail', 'friendship', ')'
   ]
```

TermQuery

To express the simplest of all queries in FQL, simply type the term you wish to find:

```
'ferret'
```

When parsed by the `QueryParser`, this string will be translated to a query that will search for the term "ferret" in all fields specified with `:default_fields` parameter.

To constrain your search to a field other than the field(s) specified by `:default_fields`, prefix your search with the field name followed by a colon. For example, if you want to search the `:title` field for the term "Ruby", you would do so like this:

```
'title:Ruby'
```

Searching multiple fields is easy, too. Simply separate field names with a | character. So, to search `:title` and `:content` fields for "Ruby", you would type:

```
'title|content:Ruby'
```

You can match all fields with the * character:

```
'*:Ruby'
```

That's all there is to specifying the field to search. If you want to search for documents that contain the term Ruby in both the `:title` and `:content` fields, you will need to use a Boolean query.

BooleanQuery

Most readers have used Boolean queries in search applications before. The most common syntax makes use of the + and - characters, + indicating terms that *must* occur and - indicating terms that *must not* occur. So, to search for documents on "Ferret" that preferably have the term "Ruby" and must not have the term "pet", you would type the following query:

```
'+Ferret Ruby -pet'
```

+ and - can also be rewritten as "REQ" and "NOT", respectively. Ferret also supports the "AND" and "OR" keywords. "AND" has precedence over "OR", but this can be overridden with the use of parentheses: `(` and `)`. So, to search for a chocolate or caramel sundae, you'd type:

```
'(chocolate OR caramel) AND sundae'
```

This could also be written as:

```
'+(chocolate caramel) +sundae'
```

It's just a matter of personal preference.

Field constraints can be applied to individual terms or whole Boolean queries wrapped in brackets:

```
'+flavour:(chocolate caramel) +name:sundae'
```

Inner field constraints override outer field constraints, so the following is equivalent to the previous query:

```
'name:(flavour:(chocolate caramel) AND sundae)'
```

PhraseQuery

As you would expect, in FQL phrase queries are identified by " characters. So, to search for the phrase "quick brown fox", your query would be just that:

```
'"quick brown fox"'
```

But Ferret phrase queries offer a lot more. You can specify a list of options for a term in a phrase. Let's say we don't care if the fox is "red", "orange", or "brown". You could search for the following phrase:

```
'"quick red|orange|brown fox"'
```

We could even accept absolutely anything in a term's position. For example, the following would match "quick hungry fox":

```
'"quick <> fox"'
```

In the "PhraseQuery" section earlier in this chapter, we also discussed sloppy phrase queries. The phrase *slop* can be indicated using the ~ character followed by an integer slop value. For example, the following query would match the phrase "quick brown and white fox":

```
'"quick fox"~3'
```

As with other types of query, phrase queries can have field constraints applied to them:

```
'content|title:"quick fox"~3'
```

RangeQuery

Range queries can be specified in a couple of different ways. The [] and {} brackets represent inclusive and exclusive limits, respectively. This syntax is inherited from the Apache Lucene query syntax. Let's say you want all documents created on or after the 25th of April, 2006, and before the 11th of November (but not on that day). You would specify the query like this:

```
'created_on:[20060425 20061111}'
```

In FQL, you can also express upper and lower bounded range queries. The open bounds are identified by the > and < tokens. For example, if I want all documents created after the 25th of July, 1977, I would write the query like this:

```
'created_on:[20060725>'
```

To find all documents created before that date, you could type this:

```
'created_on:<20060725}'
```

Alternatively, you can use the >, <, >=, and <= tokens to specify singly bounded range queries. The previous two queries would be, respectively:

```
'created_on:>= 20060725'
'created_on:< 20060725'
```

WildcardQuery

Wildcard queries in Ferret make use of the * and ? characters. Just to reiterate what we covered in the "WildcardQuery" section earlier in this chapter, * will match any number of characters, whereas ? will match a single character only. So, the following query will match all documents with the terms "lend", "legend", or "lead" in the `:content` field:

```
'content:l*e?d'
```

We can also use wildcard query syntax to create a few other types of queries. For example, to create a `MatchAllQuery`, you would type:

```
'*'
```

Note that it makes no difference if we add a field constraint to this query. To find all documents with a price field, you might be tempted to type the following:

```
'price:*'
```

But this will match all documents. Instead, you need to type the following:

```
'price:?*'
```

You can also create prefix queries using wildcard syntax. Simply type the prefix and append * to the end. For example:

```
'category:/programming/ruby/*'
```

This query will be optimized into a `PrefixQuery` by the `QueryParser`.

FuzzyQuery

In the "FuzzyQuery" section earlier in this chapter, we said that `FuzzyQueries` are to `TermQueries` as sloppy `PhraseQueries` are to standard `PhraseQueries`, so it should come as no surprise that `FuzzyQueries` use the same syntax as sloppy `PhraseQueries`. Instead of a "slop" integer, however, we have a "similarity" float, which must be between 0.0 and 1.0. Another difference is that `FuzzyQueries` have a default similarity of 0.5, so you don't need to specify a similarity value at all. Let's say, for example, that we wish to find all documents containing the commonly misspelled word "mischievous":

```
'mischievous~'
```

Or we could make the query more strict by increasing the similarity value, like this:

```
'mischievous~0.8'
```

Remember that `FuzzyQueries` are expensive queries to use on a large index, so you may want to set the default prefix length as described at the end of the "FuzzyQuery" section.

Boosting a query in FQL

Boosting queries in FQL is a simple matter of appending the query with ^ and a boost value (see the "Boosting Queries" section earlier in this chapter). For example, let's go back to our Boolean search for "Ferret" where the results included the term "Ruby" but not the term "pet". In this case, "Ferret" is the most important term, so we should boost it:

```
'+Ferret^10.0 Ruby^0.1 -pet'
```

Note that it makes no sense to boost negative clauses in a boolean query. We should also note that the boost comes after the slop in a sloppy `PhraseQuery` and the similarity in a `FuzzyQuery`:

```
'"quick brown fox"~5^10.0 AND date:>=20060601'
```

```
'mischievous~0.8^10.0 AND date:>=20060601'
```

Filtering Search Results

We've already mentioned `Filters` in our discussion of `ConstantScoreQuery` and `FilteredQuery`. `Filters` are used to apply extra constraints to a result set. For example, we want to restrict our search to documents that were created during the last month. We have two options: add a `RangeQuery` clause to our query, or apply a `RangeFilter`. The main advantage of using a `Filter` over a `Query` is that no score is taken into account, so a `Filter` can be a lot faster. To add to that, `Filters` cache their results so that subsequent uses of the `Filter` perform even better again. All caching is done against an instance of an `IndexReader`, so a new cache needs to be built each time a `Filter` is used against a different `IndexReader`.

`Filters` also make it easy to apply constraints to user input queries. `Filters` are best used when applying commonly used constraints to a user's query, such as restricting a search of a blog to only today's postings or only to postings marked for publication.

There are only two standard `Filters` that come with Ferret:

- `RangeFilter`
- `QueryFilter`

Using the RangeFilter

`RangeFilter` takes the same parameters as `RangeQuery` as described in the "RangeQuery" section earlier in this chapter. Basically, you need to supply a `:field` and an upper and/or lower limit for that field. For example, if you want to restrict a search to products that are priced at $50.00 or more and less than $100.00, we would build the filter like this:

```
price_filter = RangeFilter.new(:price, :>= => "050.00", :< => "100.00")
```

Note again the way we padded the price values. `RangeFilter` works only on fields that are correctly lexically sorted, so you need to remember to pad all number fields to a fixed width if you want to filter that field with a `RangeFilter`.

Using the QueryFilter

`QueryFilter` makes use of a query to filter search results. The initial application of a `QueryFilter` will be just as slow as if you added the filter query as a `:must` clause to the actual query. However, after caching, subsequent use of the `QueryFilter` will be much faster.

A good example of where you might use a `QueryFilter` is to restrict a search to only published articles in a CMS (Content Management System). You would create the filter like this:

```
published_filter = QueryFilter.new(TermQuery.new(:state, "published"))
```

Remember that to take full advantage of the `Filter` properties you should only create this filter once and keep a handle to it. Don't create a new `QueryFilter` every time the `search` method is invoked.

Writing Your Own Filter

Writing your own filter turns out to be pretty easy. All you need to do is implement a `bits` method, which takes an `IndexReader` and returns a `BitVector`. The best way to explain this is with an example. Let's build a `RangeFilter` that works for floats that haven't been padded to fixed width:

```
require 'rubygems'
require 'ferret'

class FloatRangeFilter
  attr_accessor :field, :upper, :lower, :upper_op, :lower_op

  def initialize(field, options)
    @field = field
    @upper = options[:<] || options[:<=]
    @lower = options[:>] || options[:>=]
    if @upper.nil? and @lower.nil?
      raise ArgError, "Must specify a bound"
    end
    @upper_op = options[:<].nil? ? :<= : :<
    @lower_op = options[:>].nil? ? :>= : :>
  end

  def bits(index_reader)
    bit_vector = Ferret::Utils::BitVector.new
    term_doc_enum = index_reader.term_docs
    index_reader.terms(@field).each do |term, freq|
      float = term.to_f
      next if @upper and not float.send(@upper_op, @upper)
      next if @lower and not float.send(@lower_op, @lower)
      term_doc_enum.seek(@field, term)
      term_doc_enum.each {|doc_id, freq| bit_vector.set(doc_id)}
    end
```

```
27      return bit_vector
28    end
29
30    def hash
31      return @field.hash ^ @upper.hash ^ @lower.hash ^
32             @upper_op.hash ^ @lower_op.hash
33    end
34
35    def eql?(o)
36      return (o.instance_of?(FloatRangeFilter) and @field == o.field and
37              @upper == o.upper and @lower == o.lower and
38              @upper_op == o.upper_op and @lower_op == o.lower_op)
39    end
40  end
```

You instantiate this by passing a field name and one or two of the optional parameters (`:<`, `:<=`, `:>`, and `:>=`) used to specify the bounds. These optional parameters should be `Floats`. The most important method in this class is the `bits` method. Starting from line 20, it iterates through all the terms in the specified field, converts the term to a `Float`, and checks that it is in the required range.

There is a little bit of trickiness on lines 22 and 23 where we are checking that the term is within the required range. `f.send(@upper_op, @upper)` translates either to `f < @upper` or to `f <= @upper`, depending on which of the less-than parameters (`:<` or `:<=`) were passed. `@upper_op` gets set on line 13.

Once we know that the term falls within the required range, the next step is to fill in the bits in the `BitVector` for all the documents in which that term appears. We do this on line 25 using a `TermDocEnum`. The final `BitVector` has a bit set for every document in the index that has a term in the specified field within the required floating-point range.

Using our new custom filter is simple. Simply pass it as the `:filter` parameter:

```
filter = FloatRangeFilter.new(:price, :< => 100.0, :>= => 10.0)
searcher.search_each("*", :filter => filter) do |d, s|
  puts "price => #{searcher[d][:price]}"
end
```

In this example, we would get all products with a price of $10.00 or more and less than $100.00.

Filter Caching Explained

You could easily stop after implementing the `bits` method and everything would work as expected. However, to make good use of `Filter` caching, you should implement `hash` and `eql?` methods. Whenever the `bits` method of a filter is called with an `IndexReader`, the `BitVector` that is returned is cached for that `IndexReader`. So, the next time the filter is used with the same

IndexReader, the cached BitVector is used. The cache is stored in a Hash, so you should implement hash and eql? methods in your custom Filter.

While we are on the topic, we should talk about the memory used by filters. If you have a million-document index, each cached BitVector is going to take 1,000,000/8 ~ 125 Kb of memory (one bit for each document in the index). Creating too many filters could lead to a memory problem. However, each cached BitVector will be destroyed when its corresponding filter or IndexReader is destroyed, so as long as you don't keep references to old filters—keeping them from being garbage-collected—you shouldn't have a problem.

:filter_proc, the New Filter

The :filter_proc parameter of the Searcher#search methods is one of the more recent additions to the Ferret arsenal. It enables you to do a lot of things that were impossible with only Filter objects. Basically, you supply a Proc object that gets called for every result in the result set. The Proc object takes three parameters: a document ID, a score, and the Searcher object. So, if you want to filter documents by geographical location, each document would need a latitude and a longitude from which you would measure the distance to a desired location:

```
0 require 'rubygems'
1 require 'ferret'
2 index = Ferret::I.new()
3 index << {:latitude => 100.0, :longitude => 100.0, :f => "close"}
4 index << {:latitude => 120.0, :longitude => 120.0, :f => "to far"}
5 index << {:latitude => 110.0, :longitude => 110.0, :f => "close"}
6 index << {:latitude => 120.0, :longitude => 100.0, :f => "close"}
7 index << {:latitude => 100.0, :longitude => 120.0, :f => "close"}
8
9 def make_distance_proc(latitude, longitude, limit)
10   Proc.new do |doc_id, score, searcher|
11     distance_2 = (searcher[doc_id][:latitude].to_f - latitude) ** 2 +
12                  (searcher[doc_id][:longitude].to_f - longitude) ** 2
13     limit_2 = limit ** 2
14     next limit_2 >= distance_2
15   end
16 end
17
18 filter_proc =  make_distance_proc(100.0, 100.0, 20.0)
19 index.search_each("*", :filter_proc => filter_proc) do |doc_id, score|
20   puts "location is #{index[doc_id][:f]}"
21 end
```

The first seven lines are just setting up the index with test data. The make_distance_proc method on line 9 creates a Proc that will check if a document falls within `limit` kilometers of the locations specified by the `latitude` and `longitude` parameters. We simply pass this `Proc` to the `search_each` method via the `:filter_proc` parameter.

Although it is called `:filter_proc`, you aren't restricted to using this parameter for filtering search results. One nifty thing you can do with a `:filter_proc` is group results from the result set:

```
 0 require 'rubygems'
 1 require 'ferret'
 2 index = Ferret::I.new()
 3 index << {:value => 1, :data => "one"}
 4 index << {:value => 2, :data => "2"}
 5 index << {:value => 3, :data => "3.0"}
 6 index << {:value => 1, :data => "1.0"}
 7 index << {:value => 3, :data => "three"}
 8 index << {:value => 2, :data => "2.0"}
 9 index << {:value => 1, :data => "1"}
10
11 results = {}
12 group_by_proc = lambda do |doc_id, score, searcher|
13   doc = searcher[doc_id]
14   (results[doc[:value]]||=[]) << doc[:data]
15   next true
16 end
17
18 index.search("*", :filter_proc => group_by_proc)
19 puts results.inspect
```

Again, the first nine lines just set up the index with test data. The `group_by_proc` created on line 12 is the interesting part, grouping documents by the `:value` field and adding the `:data` field to the `results Hash`. Obviously, this is just a silly example to demonstrate how the `:filter_proc` works. This is easily extensible to much more interesting problems.

Sorting Search Results

By default, documents are sorted by relevance and then by document ID if scores are equal. But what if we want to sort the result set by the value in one of the fields (e.g., price)? One way to do this is to retrieve the entire result set and make use of Ruby's `Array#sort` method. However, this would take too long for large result sets, not to mention use up a lot of unnecessary memory. Searcher provides a `:sort` parameter for easy sorting. The easiest way to specify a sort is to pass a sort string. A sort string is a comma-separated list of field names with an optional `DESC` modifier to reverse the sort for that field. The type of the field is automatically detected and the field sorted accordingly. So `Float` fields will be sorted by `Float` value, and `Integer` fields will be sorted by

`Integer` value. `SCORE` and `DOC_ID` can be used in place of field names to sort by relevance and internal document ID, respectively. Here are some examples:

```
index.search(query, :sort => "title, year DESC")
index.search(query, :sort => "SCORE DESC, DOC_ID DESC")
index.search(query, :sort => "SCORE, rating DESC")
```

Although this will do the job most of the time, you can be a little more explicit in describing how a result set is sorted by using the Sort API. You will also need to use the Sort API to take full advantage of sort caching. There are two classes in the Sort API: `Sort` and `SortField`.

Sort Caching Explained

As with filters, sorts are cached when they are run. That is to say, when you sort by a particular field, an index is built for it so that the next time you sort by that field, sorting will be a lot quicker. Sort indexes can take a while to build, particularly on unoptimized indexes. If you have a large index and sorting is taking too long, try optimizing the index. For a large-enough index, it can actually be quicker to optimize the index and build the sort index than to build the sort index from an unoptimized index.

Also, keep in mind the amount of memory that gets used by a sort index. Float, integer, and byte sort indexes take 4 bytes per document in the index. A string index will take that plus enough memory to store every single term in the field, including another 4-byte pointer for each term. For example, if a filesystem has 1,000,000 files, then on average the length of the `:path` field might be 20 bytes (every path is unique). If you want to sort your results by the file path, then the index would be $1{,}000{,}000 \times (4 + 20 + 4) = 28$ MB. That's a fair amount of memory for a seemingly simple task, not to mention the amount of time it would take to build such an index. Fortunately, we can do a lot better than this by using a byte sort.

SortField

A `SortField` describes how a particular field should be sorted. To create a `SortField`, you need to supply a field name and a sort type. You can also optionally reverse the sort. Table 4-2 shows the available sort types. Note that sort types are identified by `Symbols`.

Table 4-2. Sort types

Sort type	Description
`:auto`	The default type used when we supply a string sort descriptor. Ferret will look at the first term in the field's index to detect its type. It will sort the field either by integer, float, or string depending on that first term's type. Be careful when using `:auto` to sort fields that have numbers in them.

Sort type	Description
	If, for example, you are sorting a field with television show titles, "24" would probably be the first term in the index, making Ferret think that the field is an integer field.
`:integer`	Converts every term in the field to an integer and sorts by those integers.
`:float`	Converts every term in the field to a float and sorts by those floats.
`:string`	Performs a locale-sensitive sort on the field. You need to make sure you have your locale set correctly for this to work. If the locale is set to ASCII or ISO-8859-1 and the field is encoded in UTF-8, the field will be incorrectly sorted.
`:byte`	Sorts terms by the order they appear in the index. This will work perfectly for ASCII data and is a *lot* faster than a string sort.
`:doc_id`	Sorts documents by their internal document ID. For this type of `SortField`, a field name is not necessary.
`:score`	Sort documents by their relevance. This is how documents are sorted when no sort is specified. For this type of `SortField`, a field name is not necessary.

The `SortField` class also has four constant `SortField` objects:

- `SortField::SCORE`
- `SortField::DOC_ID`
- `SortField::SCORE_REV`
- `SortField::DOC_ID_REV`

With these constants available, you generally won't ever need to create a `SortField` with the type `:score` or `:doc_id`. Here are some examples of how to create `SortFields`:

```
title_sort = SortField.new(:title, :type => :string)
path_sort = SortField.new(:path, :type => :byte)
rating_sort = SortField.new(:rating, :type => :float, :reverse => true)
```

Sort

The `Sort` object is used to hold `SortFields` in order of precedence to sort a result set. It is relatively straightforward to use. It also allows you to completely reverse all `SortFields` in one go (so already reversed fields will be reversed back to normal). Here are a couple of examples:

```
title_sort = SortField.new(:title, :type => :string)
path_sort = SortField.new(:path, :type => :byte)
rating_sort = SortField.new(:rating, :type => :float, :reverse => true)

sort = Sort.new([title_sort, rating_sort, SortField::SCORE])
top_docs = index.search(query, :sort => sort)

# reverse all sort-fields.
```

```
sort = Sort.new([path_sort, SortField::DOC_ID_REV], true)
top_docs = index.search(query, :sort => sort)
```

The Sort class also has two constants: Sort::RELAVANCE and Sort::INDEX_ORDER. Sort::RELAVANCE will order fields by score as is done by default in Ferret. Sort::INDEX_ORDER sorts a result set to the order in which the documents were added to the index.

Sorting by Date

Possibly one of the most common sorts to perform is a sort by date. We discussed how to store date fields for sorting in the "Date Fields" section in Chapter 2. If you have stored the date field correctly (in YYYYMMDD format), it is very simple to sort by this field. The best sort type to use is :byte because it will be the fastest to create the index and otherwise performs just as well as aninteger sort. Using :auto, Ferret will sort the field by integer, which will be fine as well, so it is no problem using the sort string descriptor (e.g., "updated_on, created_on, DESC"). Here is how you would explicitly create a Sort to sort a date field:

```
updated_on = SortField.new(:updated_on, :type => :byte)
created_on = SortField.new(:created_on, :type => :byte, :reverse => true)
sort = Sort.new([updated_on, created_on, SortField::DOC_ID])
index.search(query, :sort => sort)
```

Highlighting Query Results

Query highlighting, like excerpting, is one of the newer features in Ferret, added in version 0.10. Highlighting takes a query and returns the data from a document field with all of the matches in the field highlighted. Excerpting, on the other hand, takes excerpts from the field, preferably with matching terms, and highlights the terms in those excerpts. Both Ferret::Search::Searcher and Ferret::Index::Index classes have a **highlight** method. In this section, we'll look at Index#**highlight** because it allows us to pass string queries instead of having to build Query objects (see Table 4-3). Otherwise, both methods are essentially the same. To use the **highlight** method, you must supply a query and the document ID of the document you wish to highlight. A number of other parameters can be used to describe exactly how you want to highlight the field.

Table 4-3. Index#highlight parameters

Parameter	Description
:field	Defaults to @options[:default_field]. The highlighter only works on one field at a time, so you need to specify which field it is you want to highlight. If you want to highlight multiple fields, you'll need to call this method multiple times.
:excerpt_length	Defaults to 150 bytes. This parameter specifies the length of excerpt to show. The algorithm for extracting excerpts attempts to fit as many matched terms into each excerpt as possible. If you'd simply like the complete field back with all matches highlighted, set this parameter to :all.
:num_excerpts	Specifies the number of excerpts you wish to retrieve. This defaults to 2, unless :excerpt_length is set to :all, in which case :num_excerpts is automatically set to 1.
:pre_tag	To highlight matches, you need to specify short strings to place before and after matches. :pre_tag defaults to <b>, which is fine when printing HTML, but if you are printing results to the console, we recommend using something like \033[36m.
:post_tag	Defaults to </b>. This tag should close whatever you specified in :pre_tag. Try tag \033[m for console applications.
:ellipsis	Defaults funnily enough to .... This is the string that is appended at the beginning and end of excerpts where the excerpts break in the middle of a field. Alternatively, you may want to use the HTML entity … or the UTF-8 string \342\200\246.

The highlight method returns an array of strings, the strings being the extracted excerpts. Example 4-1 demonstrates the flexibility of Ferret's highlighting. We store the optional parameters in a hash to avoid specifying them for each call to the highlight method. We also use a StemmingAnalyzer to demonstrate that phrases don't need to be exact to match. Don't worry about how this works just yet. You'll learn more about analysis in the next chapter.

Example 4-1. Query highlighter

```
require 'rubygems'
require 'ferret'

class MyAnalyzer < Ferret::Analysis::StandardAnalyzer
  def token_stream(field, input)
    Ferret::Analysis::StemFilter.new(super)
  end
end

index = Ferret::I.new(:analyzer => MyAnalyzer.new)

index << {
  :title => "Mark Twain Excerpts",
  :content => <<-EOF
  If it had not been for him, with his incendiary "Early to bed and
  early to rise," and all that sort of foolishness, I wouldn't have
  been so harried and worried and raked out of bed at such unseemly
```

```
    hours when I was young. The late Franklin was well enough in his
    way; but it would have looked more dignified in him to have gone on
    making candles and letting other people get up when they wanted to.
    - Letter from Mark Twain, San Francisco Alta California, July 25, 1869

    When one receives a letter from a great man for the first time in
    his life, it is a large event to him, as all of you know by your own
    experience. You never can receive letters enough from famous men
    afterward to obliterate that one, or dim the memory of the pleasant
    surprise it was, and the gratification it gave you.
    - Mark Twain's Speeches, "Unconscious Plagiarism"
  EOF
  }

  options = {
    :field => :content,
    :pre_tag => "\033[36m",
    :post_tag => "\033[m",
    :ellipsis => " \342\200\246 "
  }
  query = '"Early <> Bed" "receive letter"~1 Twain early'

  puts "_" * 60 + "\n\t*** Extract two excerpts ***\n\n"
  puts index.highlight(query, 0, options)

  puts "_" * 60 + "\n\t*** Extract four smaller excerpts ***\n\n"
  options[:num_excerpts] = 4
  options[:excerpt_length] = 50
  puts index.highlight(query, 0, options)

  puts "_" * 60 + "\n\t*** Highlight the entire field ***\n\n"
  options[:excerpt_length] = :all
  puts index.highlight(query, 0, options)
```

You'll notice here that the second example that's supposed to extract four excerpts of length 50 bytes actually extracts two excerpts of 50 bytes and one of 100 bytes. The excerpting algorithm works by attempting to place the excerpts so that the maximum number of matched terms will be shown. If it can concatenate two or more excerpts without reducing the number of matched terms shown, it will.

Summary

Now that we've covered Ferret's search API, you should know how and when to use `Queries` and `Filters`, the pros and cons of each, and when to take advantage of Ferret's `QueryParser`. You've learned how to sort your result sets and what to do about sorting performance problems. You should now be able to design the search feature of your application to best suit the needs of your users, keeping in mind the resources used by different queries, filters, and sorts.

CHAPTER 5

Analysis

Analysis is the foundation of any search library. It is the process of taking an input field and breaking it up into tokens to be added to the inverted index. So, why did we wait until now to cover this important subject? Most of the time, Ferret's standard analyzer will do exactly what you need it to do. However, when it doesn't, Ferret's analysis API is very easy to extend to your needs. To understand the analysis API, you need to know about three classes:

- `Token`
- `TokenStream`
- `Analyzer`

Token

The `Token` is the basic datatype in analysis. It is basically just a `Struct` with four attributes:

- Text
- Start offset
- End offset
- Position increment

The text attribute is obviously a `String` holding the token's text. Ferret allows tokens of up to 255 bytes long. Any longer than that and the text gets truncated to that length.

The start and end offsets hold the byte positions of the start and end of the token in the original field, the end being the byte immediately after the last byte in the token. For example, in the string "The Old Man and the Sea", the "Old" token has a start offset of 4 and an end offset of 7. The difference between the start offset and the end offset is usually equal to the length of the token's text, but not always. For example, Ferret's standard analyzer strips possessives ('s). In the field "Jamie's Kitchen", for instance, the first token will be "Jamie" but the start and end offset will be 0 and 7, respectively, also encompassing the possessive "'s". This makes it possible to extract the original token from the data source for use in tasks such as highlighting. (See Example 4-1 in the "Highlighting Query Results" section in Chapter 4 for an example of highlighting original tokens after the tokens have been processed for indexing.) The actual offsets are stored in the term vectors, so if you don't store term vectors, they are not really important.

The final attribute in `Token`—the position increment—is used to hold the number of positions that the token appears after the previous token. Most of the time, as one would expect, this is set to 1. The reason it might not be 1 is that some of the token filters remove unnecessary tokens so there will be gaps between tokens. For example, a standard English stop word filter that removes common English words like "the" and "and" will take the field "The Old Man and the Sea" and return the tokens "old", "man", and "sea" with the position increments of 2, 1, and 3, respectively. These position increments are used by Ferret to calculate the positions of the terms in the field that, in turn, are used when running phrase queries against the index, so it is important that you get these right.

TokenStream

A `TokenStream` takes a field and turns it into a list of tokens. To implement a `TokenStream`, you need to supply two methods. `TokenStream#next` should return `Tokens` in the order followed by `nil` when there are no more tokens left in the field. `TokenStream#text=` is used to set the text that the `TokenStream` will analyze. In Ferret, there are two types of `TokenStreams`: `Tokenizers` and `TokenFilters`.

In the next two sections, we'll make use of the following test code to test each `TokenStream`, printing the tokens in a table:

```
def test_token_stream(token_stream)
  puts "\033[32mStart | End | PosInc | Text\033[m"
  while t = token_stream.next
    puts "%5d |%4d |%5d   | %s" % [t.start, t.end, t.pos_inc, t.text]
  end
end
```

Tokenizer

`Tokenizers` take the raw text data from a field and turn it into a list of `Tokens`. Ferret comes with a number of tokenizer implementations, including:

- WhiteSpaceTokenizer (and AsciiWhiteSpaceTokenizer)
- LetterTokenizer (and AsciiLetterTokenizer)
- StandardTokenizer (and AsciiStandardTokenizer)
- RegExpTokenizer

Where an ASCII tokenizer exists, the non-ASCII tokenizer is locale-sensitive. That means that the tokenizer will recognize letters, numbers, and whitespace as specified by your locale. If your locale is set to UTF-8, then the tokenizer will recognize UTF-8 characters. This means you need to make sure that the data you are feeding Ferret is in the correct encoding according to your locale; otherwise, you could wind up running into some strange errors. The ASCII tokenizers tend to be more robust and a little faster than the locale-sensitive tokenizers, so if your data is ASCII, you should definitely use an ASCII analyzer.

WhiteSpaceTokenizer

The WhiteSpaceTokenizer simply recognizes tokens as strings of characters separated by whitespace. To instantiate a WhiteSpaceTokenizer, you need to pass an input string to be tokenized. You can also optionally set the tokenizer to downcase all letters. For example:

```
ts = WhiteSpaceTokenizer.new("Wally's RÉSUMÉ, at " +
                             "http://www.wally.com/ 1234", true)
test_token_stream(ts)

# Start | End | PosInc | Text
#     0 |   7 |    1   | wally's
#     8 |  17 |    1   | résumé,
#    18 |  20 |    1   | at
#    21 |  42 |    1   | http://www.wally.com/
#    43 |  47 |    1   | 1234
```

As you can see, this tokenizer works pretty well except for one problem: punctuation will be indexed with tokens. So in the previous example, a search for "wally" or "résumé" will not match, but a search for "wally's" or "résumé," will. It handles tokens such as numbers and URLs very well, though. It is also very fast.

Readers coming from a Lucene background might be surprised to see that the tokenizer is doing the downcasing, expecting that job to be left to a LowerCaseFilter. Ferret also has a LowerCaseFilter, however, WhiteSpaceTokenizer and LetterTokenizer save work by lowercasing the tokens at the same time as tokenizing. The ASCII versions of the same two tokenizers (AsciiWhiteSpaceTokenizer and AsciiLetterTokenizer) need to be wrapped in a LowerCaseFilter to downcase tokens.

> **Setting Your Locale with Ferret**
>
> Depending on your locale, you may find you get "rÉsumÉ" instead of "résumé". You can see what your current locale setting is by printing the `Ferret.locale` attribute. You can also set the same variable to set the locale. Check your system's documentation to find out the locale string that you need:
>
> ```
> # to check the locale
> puts Ferret.locale
>
> # to set the locale to American English UTF-8 on linux
> Ferret.locale = "en_US.UTF-8"
> ```

LetterTokenizer

The `LetterTokenizer` recognizes tokens as a series of letters as specified by your locale. Note that the locale "en_US.UTF-8" (or any UTF-8 locale, for that matter) will recognize characters like ß and æ, even though they are not commonly used in American English. `AsciiLetterTokenizer`, on the other hand, recognizes only the 52 characters `[a-zA-Z]`:

```
ts = LetterTokenizer.new("Wally's RÉSUMÉ, at " +
                         "http://www.wally.com/ 1234", true)
test_token_stream(ts)

# Start | End | PosInc | Text
#     0 |   5 |      1 | wally
#     6 |   7 |      1 | s
#     8 |  16 |      1 | résumé
#    18 |  20 |      1 | at
#    21 |  25 |      1 | http
#    28 |  31 |      1 | www
#    32 |  37 |      1 | wally
#    38 |  41 |      1 | com
```

We no longer have the punctuation problem we had with the `WhiteSpaceTokenizer`, but URLs are not tokenized as a single token and numbers are skipped completely. However, like the `WhiteSpaceTokenizer`, the `LetterTokenizer` is very fast and can be useful for tokenizing code.

StandardTokenizer

The `StandardTokenizer` solves the problems of the previous two analyzers—the one catch being that it is a little slower. This time there is no option to downcase the tokens, so this tokenizer needs to be wrapped in a `LowerCaseFilter` to do the lowercasing:

```
ts = StandardTokenizer.new("Wally's RÉSUMÉ, at " +
                           "http://www.wally.com/ 1234")
```

```
test_token_stream(ts)

# Start | End | PosInc | Text
#     0 |   7 |    1   | Wally
#     8 |  16 |    1   | RÉSUMÉ
#    18 |  20 |    1   | at
#    21 |  41 |    1   | www.wally.com
#    43 |  47 |    1   | 1234
```

The `StandardTokenizer` is used by Ferret's default analyzer, aptly named `StandardAnalyzer`. It should work well for most European languages.

Although `StandardTokenizer` will do the job most of the time, there are times when you need to define your own tokenizer. That's where the next tokenizer comes in handy.

RegExpTokenizer

The `RegExpTokenizer` allows you to specify a Ruby regular expression to match tokens. For example, `/\S+/` would be equivalent to the `AsciiWhiteSpaceTokenizer`, and `/[a-zA-Z]+/` would be equivalent to the `AsciiLetterTokenizer`. Unfortunately, in the current Ruby (version 1.8) regular expression implementation, the character class `[:alpha:]` will only match ASCII characters, no matter what your locale is set to. Not to worry, though; we can easily add more. Let's say we want to implement a German `LetterTokenizer` that also includes numbers. We could use the regular expression `/[[:alnum:]öÖüÜäÄß]+/`. Note that you will still need to have your locale set to use "UTF-8" for this to work:

```
ts = RegExpTokenizer.new('"Fix Schwyz!", quäkt Jürgen blöd vom Paß.',
                         /[[:alnum:]öÖüÜäÄß]+/)
test_token_stream(ts)

# Start | End | PosInc | Text
#     1 |   4 |    1   | Fix
#     5 |  11 |    1   | Schwyz
#    15 |  21 |    1   | quäkt
#    22 |  29 |    1   | Jürgen
#    30 |  35 |    1   | blöd
#    36 |  39 |    1   | vom
#    40 |  44 |    1   | Paß
```

Using the `RegExpTokenizer`, you should be able to build just about any tokenizer that you might need. Otherwise, it is pretty simple to implement a tokenizer yourself. We'll see an example of a custom tokenizer in the "Analyzer" section later in this chapter.

TokenFilter

A TokenFilter wraps a TokenStream, be it a Tokenizer or another TokenFilter, and postprocesses the tokens returned by it. The following TokenFilters come with Ferret:

- LowerCaseFilter (and AsciiLowerCaseFilter)
- StopFilter
- StemFilter
- HyphenFilter

LowerCaseFilter

The LowerCaseFilter takes a TokenStream and converts all tokens to lowercase. Again, you need to be certain you have your locale set correctly. If the locale does not match the encoding of your data, then LowerCaseFilter won't work correctly. The AsciiLowerCaseFilter does the same job, except that it won't work on non-ASCII characters. This filter must be applied to the TokenStream before StopFilter and StemFilter will work. Even if you don't use either of these filters, you should probably use LowerCaseFilter anyway.

Earlier when we introduced StandardTokenizer, we showed that it couldn't downcase its tokens. We'll remedy that now:

```
ts = StandardTokenizer.new("Wally's RÉSUMÉ, at " +
                           "http://www.wally.com/ 1234")
ts = LowerCaseFilter.new(ts)
test_token_stream(ts)

# Start | End | PosInc | Text
#     0 |   7 |    1   | wally
#     8 |  16 |    1   | résumé
#    18 |  20 |    1   | at
#    21 |  41 |    1   | www.wally.com
#    43 |  47 |    1   | 1234
```

StopFilter

The StopFilter can be used to filter stop words from the token stream. Stop words are common words such as "the" and "and" that aren't of much use when performing searches on the index. In a large index, you will save a lot of space and improve search performance be removing stop words. There will, however, be a slight loss in precision for some searches, so you may benefit from not using a StopFilter if you find performance isn't an issue. Here is an example of a StopFilter used on English data:

```
ts = StandardTokenizer.new("The Old Man and the Sea")
ts = StopFilter.new(LowerCaseFilter.new(ts))
```

```
test_token_stream(ts)

# Start | End | PosInc | Text
#     4 |   7 |   2    | old
#     8 |  11 |   1    | man
#    20 |  23 |   3    | sea
```

As you can see, the words "the" and "and" have been stripped from the token stream. Also note the values in the position increment column; this is the first time they haven't all been 1. "old" has a position increment of 2 because the previous "the" was removed. "man" comes straight after "old", so its position increment is 1.

Note that we filtered the data through a `LowerCaseFilter` before filtering it with `StopFilter`. If we didn't do this, "the" would have been filtered out but "The" wouldn't have been. You should always apply a `LowerCaseFilter` before applying a `StopFilter`. If you are working in a language other than English, you can supply your own list of stop words. Ferret comes with the following stop word lists:

- `Analysis::ENGLISH_STOP_WORDS`
- `Analysis::FULL_ENGLISH_STOP_WORDS`
- `Analysis::EXTENDED_ENGLISH_STOP_WORDS`
- `Analysis::FULL_FRENCH_STOP_WORDS`
- `Analysis::FULL_SPANISH_STOP_WORDS`
- `Analysis::FULL_PORTUGUESE_STOP_WORDS`
- `Analysis::FULL_ITALIAN_STOP_WORDS`
- `Analysis::FULL_GERMAN_STOP_WORDS`
- `Analysis::FULL_DUTCH_STOP_WORDS`
- `Analysis::FULL_SWEDISH_STOP_WORDS`
- `Analysis::FULL_NORWEGIAN_STOP_WORDS`
- `Analysis::FULL_DANISH_STOP_WORDS`
- `Analysis::FULL_RUSSIAN_STOP_WORDS`
- `Analysis::FULL_FINNISH_STOP_WORDS`

Here is an example of using a `StopFilter` in German, using the same Hemingway title we used previously:

```
ts = StandardTokenizer.new("Der alte Mann und das Meer")
ts = StopFilter.new(LowerCaseFilter.new(ts), FULL_GERMAN_STOP_WORDS)
test_token_stream(ts)

# Start | End | PosInc | Text
#     4 |   8 |   2    | alte
```

```
#      9 |  13 |     1    | mann
#     22 |  26 |     3    | meer
```

An English `StopFilter` is used by the default analyzer, so be sure to set it up to use the stop word list for your language.

StemFilter

Stemming is the process of breaking a word down to its morphological root. For example, "searches" and "searching" are both reduced to "search". Stemming can greatly improve the recall of your search index. For example, a search for "running magazines" will also pick up documents with the phrase "runners magazine":

```
ts = StandardTokenizer.new("Stems stemming stemmed stem")
ts = StemFilter.new(LowerCaseFilter.new(ts))
test_token_stream(ts)

# Start | End | PosInc | Text
#     0 |   5 |    1   | stem
#     6 |  14 |    1   | stem
#    15 |  22 |    1   | stem
#    23 |  27 |    1   | stem
```

You may notice that the start and end offsets indicate the start and end of the original terms, not the start and end of the stem. This is important for processes such as highlighting that need the start and end of the original term.

Ferret uses Martin Porter's Snowball stemmer (*http://snowball.tartarus.org/*), which uses the Porter stemming algorithm to stem English. The Snowball stemmer also comes with support for a number of other languages and encodings (see Table 5-1).

Table 5-1. Stemming algorithms

Algorithm	Algorithm pseudonyms	Encoding
"danish",	"da", "dan"	"ISO_8859_1", "UTF_8"
"dutch",	"dut", "nld"	"ISO_8859_1", "UTF_8"
"english",	"en", "eng"	"ISO_8859_1", "UTF_8"
"finnish",	"fi", "fin"	"ISO_8859_1", "UTF_8"
"french",	"fr", "fra", "fre"	"ISO_8859_1", "UTF_8"
"german",	"de", "deu", "ge", "ger"	"ISO_8859_1", "UTF_8"
"italian",	"it", "ita"	"ISO_8859_1", "UTF_8"
"norwegian",	"nl", "no"	"ISO_8859_1", "UTF_8"
"porter",		"ISO_8859_1", "UTF_8"
"portuguese",	"por", "pt"	"ISO_8859_1", "UTF_8"

Algorithm	Algorithm pseudonyms	Encoding
"russian",	"ru", "rus"	"KOI8_R", "UTF_8"
"spanish",	"es", "esl"	"ISO_8859_1", "UTF_8"
"swedish",	"sv", "swe"	"ISO_8859_1", "UTF_8"

The default Algorithm is English and the default Encoding is "UTF_8". Here is an example using the "russian" algorithm:

```
ts = StandardTokenizer.new("важная важнее важнейшие важнейшими важничал")
ts = StemFilter.new(LowerCaseFilter.new(ts), "ru", "UTF_8")
test_token_stream(ts)

# Start | End | PosInc | Text
#      0|  12 |    1   | важн
#     13|  25 |    1   | важн
#     26|  44 |    1   | важн
#     45|  65 |    1   | важн
#     66|  82 |    1   | важнича
```

HyphenFilter

Hyphens can be quite problematic to deal with in information retrieval. For example, a search for the term "e-mail" should match "e-mail" and "email", while the term "set-up" should match "set-up", "set up", and even "setup". The hyphenation filter does its best to handle hyphenated terms.

The hyphenated terms are concatenated and also added as distinct terms. The position increment for the term "set" is equal to 0 because it is in the same position as the term "set-up". This means that searches for "setup", "set-up", and "set up" will all match, as will the phrases "set up script" and "set-up script". Unfortunately, "setup script" will not match, but we could save this by giving the phrase a slop of 1 (i.e., "setup script"~1). See the "PhraseQuery" section in Chapter 4 for information on `PhraseQuery#slop`.

Analyzer

An `Analyzer` is basically a `TokenStream` Factory that builds `TokenStreams` specific to each field. To implement an `Analyzer`, you simply need to supply a `token_stream` method that accepts the following parameters:

`field_name`
: The name of the field to be tokenized (as a symbol)

`input`
: The text to be tokenized

Ferret comes with a number of built-in `Analyzers`:

- WhiteSpaceAnalyzer (and AsciiWhiteSpaceAnalyzer)
- LetterAnalyzer (and AsciiLetterAnalyzer)
- RegExpAnalyzer
- StandardAnalyzer (and AsciiStandardAnalyzer)
- PerFieldAnalyzer

The first three are basically wrappers for their respective tokenizers, so we won't cover them here except to mention that they are all lowercasing by default.

StandardAnalyzer

The easiest way to describe StandardAnalyzer is to show what it would look like in Ruby code:

```
module Ferret::Analysis
  class StandardAnalyzer
    def initialize(stop_words = ENGLISH_STOP_WORDS, lower = true)
      @lower = lower
      @stop_words = stop_words
    end

    def token_stream(field, str)
      ts = StandardTokenizer.new(str)
      ts = LowerCaseFilter.new(ts) if @lower
      ts = StopFilter.new(ts, @stop_words)
      ts = HyphenFilter.new(ts)
    end
  end
end
```

The first thing you will probably notice is that StandardAnalyzer uses an English list of stop words. If you are indexing in a different language, then you will probably want to use a different list of stop words. If you don't want to use a StopFilter at all, you can either build a custom Analyzer or pass an empty Array as the stop words parameter:

```
analyzer = StandardAnalyzer.new([])
```

Otherwise, the StandardAnalyzer is pretty straightforward. The code should give you a good idea of how you would go about implementing your own custom Analyzer.

PerFieldAnalyzer

The PerFieldAnalyzer allows you to assign a different analyzer for each field in your documents. Remember to use Symbols for your field names:

```
analyzer = PerFieldAnalyzer.new(StandardAnalyzer.new)
analyzer[:code_segment] = LetterAnalyzer.new
analyzer[:date] = WhiteSpaceAnalyzer.new
```

When you instantiate the PerFieldAnalyzer, you need to set the default Analyzer to be used on fields that you don't specify an analyzer for. After that, a PerFieldAnalyzer can be accessed like a Hash to get and set the Analyzers for different fields. You'll see another example of its use in the next section.

Custom Analysis

The Tokenizers and Analyzers that come with Ferret cater to most needs most of the time. However, there may come a time when Ferret's standard Analysis classes fall short and you need to implement your own. In the following example, we'll show you how to build an Analyzer that automatically pads numbers to a fixed width so that they will be correctly sorted for use with a RangeQuery or RangeFilter:

```
module Ferret::Analysis
  class IntegerTokenizer
    def initialize(num, width)
      @num = num.to_i
      @width = width
    end
    def next
      token = Token.new("%0#{@width}d" % @num, 0, @width) if @num
      @num = nil
      return token
    end
    def text=(text)
      @num = text.to_i
    end
  end

  class IntegerAnalyzer
    def initialize(width)
      @width = width
    end
    def token_stream(field, input)
      return IntegerTokenizer.new(input, @width)
    end
  end
end

include Ferret::Analysis

analyzer = PerFieldAnalyzer.new(StandardAnalyzer.new)
analyzer[:padded] = IntegerAnalyzer.new(5)

index = Ferret::I.new(:analyzer => analyzer)
[5, 50, 500, 5000, 50000].each do |number|
```

```
  index << {:padded => number, :unpadded => number}
end

puts "padded: " + index.search('padded:[10 10000]').to_s
puts "unpadded: " + index.search('unpadded:[10 10000]').to_s
```

If you run this example, you'll see that the `RangeQuery` worked on the `:padded_num` field, even though you didn't explicitly pad the numbers as you added them to the field or the numbers in the `RangeQuery` itself. The `:num` field query, on the other hand, failed miserably.

In this chapter, we have covered analysis: the processing of text for insertion into the index. Getting this right can make a big difference in the quality of search results returned to the user, and can also have an impact on the performance of both searching and indexing. You should now be able to combine Ferret's `Tokenizers` and `TokenFilters` to create the perfect `Analyzer` for your application. If Ferret's built-in `Tokenizers` and `TokenFilters` don't quite do what you need, it shouldn't be too difficult to build a custom `Analyzer` to do exactly what you want.

CHAPTER 6

Ferret in Practice

In Chapter 1, you saw how to index all the text files under a directory. Unfortunately, most of the files in a filesystem aren't text files, so let's extend the indexer to handle some different file types. We also want to filter and sort files by different fields, such as their modification date. In this chapter, we'll implement these extensions and more. We'll call our application *ferretfind*.

Indexing Multiple Document Types

```
module FerretFind
  class Reader
    @@subclasses = []
    @@readers = {}

    def Reader.inherited(subclass)
      @@subclasses << subclass
    end

    def Reader.load_readers(field_infos)
      @@subclasses.each do |subclass|
        reader = subclass.new(field_infos)
        subclass::EXTENSIONS.each do |ext|
          @@readers[ext.downcase] = reader
        end
      end
    end

    def Reader.get_reader(path)
      @@readers[(File.extname(path)[/[^.]+/]||"").downcase]
    end

    def Reader.read(path)
      document = {
        :path     => path,
        :accessed => File.atime(path).strftime("%Y%m%d"),
        :modified => File.mtime(path).strftime("%Y%m%d")
```

```
34       }
35       if File.readable?(path) and reader = Reader.get_reader(path)
36         document.merge!(reader.read(path))
37       end
38       return document
39     end
40 
41     protected
42       def initialize(field_infos); end
43       def read(path); {} end
44       def add_field(field_infos, field, options)
45         field_infos.add_field(field, options) unless field_infos[field]
46       end
47   end
48 end
```

The `FerretFind::Reader` class is an abstract class that is not meant to be instantiated. Instead, its `Reader.read` method (on line 29) is used to read documents; it adds the basic fields—`:path`, `:accessed`, and `:modified`, which can be determined for any document type—offloading the real work to the appropriate subclass. The methods that subclasses must implement are `initialize` and `read` (on lines 42 and 43).

As you can see, the `read` method accepts a path string and returns a `Hash`. At first, one might expect this method simply to return a `String` to be added to the index in the `:content` field. This would make sense for a simple text file, but there are some documents where we will want to add more than one field. For example, as you'll see in the "JpegReader" section later in this chapter, we may want to add a number of different fields that we extracted from EXIF tags.

That should explain why the `Reader#initialize` method accepts a `FieldInfos` object as a parameter. We don't know before the subreaders are loaded which fields are going to exist in the database. Each subreader will add the appropriate fields associated with it when it is instantiated. Since fields can be added only once to a `FieldInfos` object, we'll use the `Reader#add_field` (44) helper method to safely add fields to the index.

The next question is: how does the `Reader` class know which subreaders are available and which to use for each document type? Ruby classes have the nifty `inherited` method, which gets called every time a class is subclassed. We simply add all subclasses to an `Array`. Another class method `Reader.load_readers` (16) gets called after all subreaders have been loaded by the Ruby interpreter. Each reader instance is added to the `@@readers` `Hash` according to the file type it is designed to read. Therefore, each subreader is also required to define an `EXTENSIONS` constant, which must be an `Array` of file extensions.

Now that we have a way of determining the file type, we use the `Reader.get_reader` method (25) to get the correct reader based on the file extension. This method is called for all nondirectory files in the `Reader.read` method on 35.

File Type Detection

You may be a bit dubious about using a file's extension to determine its type. A better solution might be to use the *nix `file` utility to determine a file's MIME type. Alternatively, you could have each subreader implement a `Reader#can_read?(path)` method. The `Reader` class would then scan through all subreaders for each file until it found a reader that could read the file.

Let's now take a look at how this class is used. We store all subreaders in the `readers` directory next to the `ferretfind` file. Here is the code used to load readers and set up the index:

```
116   include Ferret::Index
117   readers_dir = File.join(File.dirname(__FILE__), "readers", "*.rb")
118   Dir[readers_dir].each {|fn| require fn}
119   field_infos = FieldInfos.new(:index => :untokenized_omit_norms,
120                                :term_vector => :no)
121   field_infos.add_field(:content, :store => :no, :index => :yes)
122   FerretFind::Reader.load_readers(field_infos)
123   writer = IndexWriter.new(:path => options.path,
124                            :field_infos => field_infos,
125                            :create => options.create)
```

The first thing we do on line 118 is load all readers in the `readers` directory. The subclasses will subsequently be loaded into the `Reader.subclasses Array`. Next, we create the `FieldInfos` object on 119. By default, we'll leave fields untokenized since most extra fields will be short information fields such as date fields. We also omit norms because we won't be boosting any of these fields and we want to save space. For that same reason, we don't store term vectors. Since we could potentially be indexing all the files in our filesystem, we need to save space wherever we can. When we add the `:content` field on the next line, we set `:store` to `:no`. If you would like to add fast highlighting, you will need to set `:store` to `:yes` and `:term_vector` to `:with_positions_offsets`. Keep in mind that the index will possibly take up more disk space than all the files you index combined. This won't always be the case, as most of the files on your system may be multimedia files that don't actually have a `:content` field to highlight.

On 122, we load all readers, setting up the `field_infos` object with all the possible fields. On the next line, we create an `IndexWriter` with these objects. Don't worry about the `options` variable right now—we'll go over that later. If the index already exists, the `:field_infos` parameter will be ignored, so you may need to reindex if you add or change any of the readers.

It's now time to implement some subreaders. We'll only cover a few file types here, but we hope it will give you a good idea of how you would extend this API for any file type.

TextReader

The most basic of all readers is the `TextReader`. We were already reading text files in the Chapter 1 example, so Example 6-1 isn't really anything new.

Example 6-1. ff/readers/text.rb

```
module FerretFind
  class TextReader < Reader
    EXTENSIONS = ['txt']

    def read(path)
      return {:content => File.read(path), :type => "TEXT"}
    end
  end
end
```

There is no need to implement an `initialize` method here, since we are not adding any extra fields. Note also that `EXTENSIONS` is an `Array`, even though it only handles one extension.

HtmlReader

Things get a little trickier when reading HTML. First, we need to extract the text from the HTML tags and we want to handle badly formed HTML. This counts REXML out. Fortunately, Hpricot is a great new library developed by *why the lucky stiff* (*http://code.whytheluckystiff.net/hpricot/*) that fits the bill perfectly. It can be easily installed as a gem on both Windows and *nix systems. It will also happily parse XML files should we need it to:

```
dave$ sudo gem install hpricot
```

Now that we have an HTML parser that will handle pretty much anything we throw at it, we need to decide what to store. Obviously, we would like to extract all the text and add it to the content field. We can also extract a title field from most HTML files, and it might be useful to store all of the hyperlinks in the file (although we're mostly just trying to demonstrate the utility of Hpricot). See Example 6-2.

Example 6-2. ff/readers/html.rb

```
require 'rubygems'
require 'hpricot'
```

```
module FerretFind
  class HtmlReader < Reader
    EXTENSIONS = ['htm', 'html', 'xhtml', 'rhtml']

    def initialize(field_infos)
      add_field(field_infos, :title,  :index => :yes)
    end

    def read(path)
      content = ""
      doc = Hpricot.parse(File.read(path))
      doc.traverse_text do |text_elem|
        text = text_elem.to_s.strip
        content << "#{text}\n" unless text.empty?
      end
      title = doc.at('title')
      title = title ? title.inner_html.to_s : "No Title"
      {
        :type => "HTML",
        :content => content,
        :title => title,
        :links => get_links(doc)
      }
    end

    LINK_ATTR = {
      'base'        => ['href'],
      'a'           => ['href'],
      'area'        => ['href'],
      'link'        => ['href'],
      'img'         => ['src', 'usemap', 'longdesc'],
      'q'           => ['cite'],
      'blockquote'  => ['cite'],
      'ins'         => ['cite'],
      'del'         => ['cite'],
      'form'        => ['action'],
      'input'       => ['src', 'usemap'],
      'head'        => ['profile'],
      'script'      => ['src', 'for']
    }

    def get_links(doc)
      links = []
      doc.traverse_element(*LINK_ATTR.keys) do |elem|
        LINK_ATTR[elem.name].each do |attr|
          if hyperlink = elem.get_attribute(attr)
            links << hyperlink
          end
        end
      end
      links
    end
```

```
55   end
56 end
```

This time, we do need to implement an `initialize` method because we are adding a `:title` field to the index and we would like that field to be tokenized. On line 8 where we add the `:title` field, you can see we set `:index` to `:yes`.

The `HtmlReader#read` method is fairly straightforward. On line 13, we load the HTML file into an `Hpricot::Doc`. Then on line 14, we extract all the text from the document. From line 18 we extract the title from the document. Finally, we grab all links from the document using the `HtmlReader#get_links` method (line 44). This method looks a little complex, but basically what it is doing is traversing all elements that might have a link attribute and checking each of those attributes for a link. Note that the links field is actually an `Array`. This is a good example of where it is useful to add an `Array` as a field. You can now read the document from the index and get the `Array` of links straight from the loaded Ferret document without having to parse the field.

OOoReader (OpenOffice.org Reader)

Some of the more useful document types to index are office documents. It is usually much easier to work with open file formats like those used by OpenOffice.org rather than proprietary formats (e.g., Microsoft Office), so we'll be using OpenOffice.org in this example. Later in this chapter, we'll look at a way to extract text from Microsoft Word documents.

So how do we extract text from OpenOffice.org documents? Unfortunately, no library does exactly that, but with a combination of the rubyzip project and Hpricot, we can get what we need. (Actually, this time REXML would have been sufficient, but we've got Hpricot now and it makes things much simpler.) First, we need to get the rubyzip gem (rubyzip is developed by Technorama Ltd. and Thomas Sondergaard and can be found at *http://rubyforge.org/projects/rubyzip/*):

```
dave$ sudo gem install rubyzip
```

An OpenOffice.org document is basically a group of XML documents zipped into a single file. We use rubyzip to unzip the document file, then we extract all the text from the *content.xml* file using Hpricot, just as we did for `HtmlReader`. See Example 6-3.

Example 6-3. ff/readers/ooo.rb

```
require 'rubygems'
require 'zip/zipfilesystem'
require 'hpricot'

module FerretFind
```

```
  class OOoReader < Reader
    EXTENSIONS = ['odt']

    def read(path)
      content = ""
      Zip::ZipFile.open(path) do |zip_file|
        doc = Hpricot.parse(zip_file.read('content.xml'))
        doc.traverse_text do |text_elem|
          text = text_elem.to_s.strip
          content << "#{text}\n" unless text.empty?
        end
      end
      return {:content => content, :type => "OOo"}
    end
  end
end
```

JpegReader

Now let's have a look at some binary files. Usually, you wouldn't really think about using text search to find images. However, we can extract a lot of information from JPEG files' stored EXIF tags. See Example 6-4.

> EXIF is just one tagging format we can use. We use EXIF here because there is a nice Ruby library to read EXIF tags. It would be nice to be able to just as easily read IPTC tags as well.

We'll use exifr to read the tags (exifr is developed by Remco van 't Veer; visit *http://rubyforge.org/projects/exifr/*). To install exifr:

```
dave$ sudo gem install exifr
```

Example 6-4. ff/readers/images.rb

```
require 'rubygems'
require 'exifr'

module FerretFind
  class JpegReader < Reader
    EXTENSIONS = ['jpeg', 'jpg']

    def initialize(field_infos)
      add_field(field_infos, :make, :index => :yes)
      add_field(field_infos, :model, :index => :yes)
      add_field(field_infos, :image_description, :index => :yes)
    end

    def read(path)
      begin
        jpg = EXIFR::JPEG.new(path)
```

```
      rescue Exception => e
        return {}
      end
      document = {
        :type    => "JPEG"
        :content => jpg.comment,
        :height  => jpg.height,
        :width   => jpg.width,
      }
      if jpg.exif
        document[:make]              = jpg.exif.make
        document[:model]             = jpg.exif.model
        document[:image_description] = jpg.exif.image_description
        if jpg.exif.date_time
          document[:date_taken]      = jpg.exif.date_time.strftime("%Y%m%d")
        end
      end
      document
    end
  end
end
```

Again, we add a few fields that need to be tokenized, so we set these fields up in the `initialize` method. In the `read` method, we simply choose the fields we wish to index and add them to the document. You should look at the EXIF tags stored in your photos and decide which fields you would like to index.

Mp3Reader

For good measure, let's look at another very common binary file format. MP3 information is usually stored in ID3 tags, and we can use id3lib-ruby to read these tags (id3lib-ruby is developed by Robin Stocker; check out *http://id3lib-ruby.rubyforge.org/*). As usual, there is a gem available. On Windows, it is a simple matter of installing the gem as you normally would. On other systems, you need to make sure you have id3lib installed. On Ubuntu, you can do this like so:

```
dave$ sudo apt-get install id3lib
dave$ sudo gem install id3lib-ruby
```

Once you have the correct library installed, implementing `Mp3Reader` is pretty much the same as implementing `JpegReader`. See Example 6-5.

Example 6-5. ff/readers/mp3.rb

```
require 'rubygems'
require 'id3lib'

module FerretFind
  class Mp3Reader < Reader
    EXTENSIONS = ['mp3']
```

```

    def initialize(field_infos)
      add_field(field_infos, :title,  :index => :yes)
      add_field(field_infos, :artist, :index => :yes)
      add_field(field_infos, :album,  :index => :yes)
    end

    def read(path)
      tag = ID3Lib::Tag.new(path)
      document = {
        :type   => "MP3",
        :artist => tag.artist,
        :title  => tag.title,
        :album  => tag.album,
      }
    end
  end
end
```

One thing to note here: sometimes `tag.artist` or one of the other tags will be nil. Adding nil fields won't hurt at all. They will just be ignored.

PdfReader

Unfortunately, there are currently no good libraries in Ruby for reading PDF files. Not to worry, though, as there are other solutions. One solution is to use the *nix utility pdftotext. See Example 6-6.

Example 6-6. ff/readers/pdf.rb

```
module FerretFind
  class PdfReader < Reader
    EXTENSIONS = ['pdf']

    def read(path)
      document = {:type => "PDF"}
      %x{pdftotext '#{path}' '#{/tmp/ferretfind.txt}' 2>/dev/null}
      if $?.exitstatus == 127
        warn 'pdftotext(1) missing'
      elsif $?.exitstatus != 0
        warn "failed converting pdf file: #{path}"
      else
        document[:content] = File.read('/tmp/ferretfind.txt')
      end
    end
  end
end
```

But what if you are on Windows or you can't get pdftotext on your system? One alternative is to write a pdftotext-like application using Java and its excellent PDFBox library. You would use it in exactly the same way.

This same technique can be used to extract text from Microsoft Word documents using the antiword utility (antiword is developed by Adri van Os; visit *http://www.winfield.demon.nl/*).

Other Indexing Improvements

Now that we can index multiple different types of documents, it would be nice to be able to have a bit more control over the indexing process. We should be able to specify multiple directories to add, and also specify file path patterns. It would also be nice if we could somehow make sure that files are added only when they need to be—e.g., either they haven't been added yet or they were modified since they were added. We'd also like some way to update the index so that modified files are reindexed and deleted files are deleted from the index.

To implement these requirements, we use Ruby's DBM class to record the time each file was added to the index. DBM is basically a storable `Hash`, which we will store in the */path/to/index/added_at* file. Note that since the filename *added_at* doesn't begin with an underscore, it won't conflict with any of the index files. It makes sense to store it in the same place as the rest of the index files, since it is basically just another index file. Here is the code used to add files to the index:

```
if not options.add.empty?
  include Ferret::Index
  readers_dir = File.join(File.dirname(__FILE__), "readers", "*.rb")
  Dir[readers_dir].each {|fn| require fn}
  field_infos = FieldInfos.new(:index => :untokenized_omit_norms,
                               :term_vector => :no)
  field_infos.add_field(:content, :store => :no, :index => :yes)
  FerretFind::Reader.load_readers(field_infos)
  writer = IndexWriter.new(:path => options.path,
                           :field_infos => field_infos,
                           :create => options.create)
  added_at = DBM.open(File.join(options.path, 'added_at'))
  count = 0
  options.add.each do |dir_path|
    dir_path = File.join(dir_path, "**/*") if File.directory?(dir_path)
    Dir[dir_path].each do |path|
      path = File.expand_path(path)
      next if added_at[path]
      count += 1
      begin; print "."; STDOUT.flush end if count % 100 == 0
      added_at[path] = Time.now._dump
      writer << FerretFind::Reader.read(path)
    end
  end
  puts "optimizing"
  writer.optimize
  puts "added #{count} documents to the index."
```

```
142   puts "There are now #{writer.doc_count} documents in the index."
143 end
```

We looked at lines 116 to 125 earlier in the "Indexing Multiple Document Types" section. Next, on 126, we open the `added_at` DBM, which contains the added times for all the files in the index. Again, don't worry too much about the `options` variable at this stage. You only need to know that `options.path` holds the path to the index, and `options.add` holds an array of directories to add to the index. Much of the subsequent code is simple logging so that the user knows that something is happening during the indexing process. The next important line to note is 132, where we skip documents that have already been added. Don't bother checking for out-of-date files in this section; the update section will take care of that. If we do index a file, we need to store the time that file was indexed, which happens on 135 before adding the document to the index on 136.

Note the optimize on line 140. This is very important in an application like this because searches will be run from the command line and the index will need to be read in from scratch each time. This will be much slower for unoptimized indexes. Now, let's take a look at the update code:

```
144 if options.update
145   writer = Ferret::Index::IndexWriter.new(:path => options.path)
146   added_at = DBM.open(File.join(options.path, 'added_at'))
147   added_at.keys.each do |path|
148     if not File.exists?(path)
149       writer.delete(:path, path)
150       added_at.delete(path)
151     elsif File.mtime(path) > Time._load(added_at[path])
152       writer.delete(:path, path)
153       writer << FerretFind::Reader.read(path)
154       added_at[path] = Time.now._dump
155     end
156   end
157 end
```

For each of the keys in `added_at` we check if the file has been deleted (line 148) or updated (line 151) and modify the index accordingly. Note the way we also need to update the `added_at` DBM in both cases.

Search Improvements

We'd like to be able to sort searches. This is pretty simple, since we can actually just pass sort strings as the `:sort` parameter to the `Index#search_each` method. We'll also give the option to specify the `:limit` and `:offset` parameters so that the user can page through search results. Here is the search code:

```
158 if options.query
159   index = Ferret::I.new(:path => options.path,
```

```
160                          :default_field => :content)
161   total = index.search_each(options.query,
162                             :limit => options.limit,
163                             :offset => options.offset,
164                             :sort => options.sort) do |id, score|
165     doc = index[id]
166     puts "%1.5f => %s" % [score, doc[:path]]
167     options.fields.each do |field|
168       puts "\t#{field} => #{doc[field]}" if doc[field]
169     end
170   end
171   start = options.offset
172   finish = [options.offset + options.limit, total].min
173   puts "** #{start}-#{finish} of #{total} documents found **"
174 end
```

We use an `Index` object here instead of a `Searcher` combined with an `IndexReader` and `QueryParser` simply because it is so much easier and does everything we need without a loss in performance. For each hit, we print the score and the `:path` field (166). We also allow the optional printing of other fields from the hits (167).

Putting It All Together

The next step is to parse the options. None of this code is really relevant to our study of Ferret right now. It is simply an example of using the *getoptlong* and *ostruct* standard libraries. For the sake of completeness, though, we'll show the whole of ferretfind here. If you are interested, the option parsing code is from 49 to 114:

```
 0 #!/usr/bin/env ruby
 1 require 'rubygems'
 2 require 'ferret'
 3 require 'optparse'
 4 require 'ostruct'
 5 require 'dbm'
 6 
 7 module FerretFind
 8   class Reader
 9     @@subclasses = []
10     @@readers = {}
11 
12     def Reader.inherited(subclass)
13       @@subclasses << subclass
14     end
15 
16     def Reader.load_readers(field_infos)
17       @@subclasses.each do |subclass|
18         reader = subclass.new(field_infos)
19         subclass::EXTENSIONS.each do |ext|
20           @@readers[ext.downcase] = reader
```

```
        end
      end
    end

    def Reader.get_reader(path)
      @@readers[(File.extname(path)[/[^.]+/]||"").downcase]
    end

    def Reader.read(path)
      document = {
        :path     => path,
        :accessed => File.atime(path).strftime("%Y%m%d"),
        :modified => File.mtime(path).strftime("%Y%m%d")
      }
      if File.readable?(path) and reader = Reader.get_reader(path)
        document.merge!(reader.read(path))
      end
      return document
    end

    protected
      def initialize(field_infos); end
      def read(path); {} end
      def add_field(field_infos, field, options)
        field_infos.add_field(field, options) unless field_infos[field]
      end
  end
end
options = OpenStruct.new
opts = OptionParser.new do |opts|
  opts.banner = "Usage: #{__FILE__} [options]"
  options.add = []
  options.path = 'index'
  options.fields = []
  options.limit = 1000
  options.offset = 0

  opts.on("-u", "--update",
          "update all modified documents in the index") do
    options.update = true
  end
  opts.on("-a", "--add </path/to/dir/**/*>",
          "add all files in directory. * matches",
          "any character so c* matches all files",
          "beginning with c. ** matches directories",
          "recursively.") do |path|
    options.add << path
  end
  opts.on("-q", "--q <query_string>",
          "Query string. You can use Ferret Query",
          "Language to submit any type of query") do |query|
    options.query = query
  end
  opts.on("-s", "--sort <sort_string>",
```

```
          "comma separated list of fields to sort by",
          "(followed by DESC to reverse sort)") do |sort|
    options.sort = sort
  end
  opts.on("-d", "--dir </path/to/index>",
          "Defaults to ./index") do |path|
    options.path = path
  end
  opts.on("-f", "--field <field>",
          "field you wish to display") do |field|
    options.fields << field.intern
  end
  opts.on("-l", "-n", "--limit <number>",
          "--num <number>", Integer,
          "number of docs you wish to display") do |limit|
    options.limit = limit
  end
  opts.on("-o", "--offset <number>", Integer,
          "offset of documents you wish to display",
          "used to page through results") do |offset|
    options.offset = offset
  end
  opts.on("-c", "--create",
          "overwrite any existing index") do
    options.create = true
  end
  opts.separator ""
  opts.separator "Common options:"
  opts.on_tail("-h", "--help", "Show this message") do
    puts opts
    exit
  end
end

opts.parse!(ARGV)
if options.add.empty? and not options.query and not options.update
  # no command used so show the usage message and exit
  puts opts
  exit
end
if not options.add.empty?
  include Ferret::Index
  readers_dir = File.join(File.dirname(__FILE__), "readers", "*.rb")
  Dir[readers_dir].each {|fn| require fn}
  field_infos = FieldInfos.new(:index => :untokenized_omit_norms,
                               :term_vector => :no)
  field_infos.add_field(:content, :store => :no, :index => :yes)
  FerretFind::Reader.load_readers(field_infos)
  writer = IndexWriter.new(:path => options.path,
                           :field_infos => field_infos,
                           :create => options.create)
  added_at = DBM.open(File.join(options.path, 'added_at'))
  count = 0
  options.add.each do |dir_path|
```

```
    dir_path = File.join(dir_path, "**/*") if File.directory?(dir_path)
    Dir[dir_path].each do |path|
      path = File.expand_path(path)
      next if added_at[path]
      count += 1
      begin; print "."; STDOUT.flush end if count % 100 == 0
      added_at[path] = Time.now._dump
      writer << FerretFind::Reader.read(path)
    end
  end
  puts "optimizing"
  writer.optimize
  puts "added #{count} documents to the index."
  puts "There are now #{writer.doc_count} documents in the index."
end
if options.update
  writer = Ferret::Index::IndexWriter.new(:path => options.path)
  added_at = DBM.open(File.join(options.path, 'added_at'))
  added_at.keys.each do |path|
    if not File.exists?(path)
      writer.delete(:path, path)
      added_at.delete(path)
    elsif File.mtime(path) > Time._load(added_at[path])
      writer.delete(:path, path)
      writer << FerretFind::Reader.read(path)
      added_at[path] = Time.now._dump
    end
  end
end
if options.query
  index = Ferret::I.new(:path => options.path,
                        :default_field => :content)
  total = index.search_each(options.query,
                            :limit => options.limit,
                            :offset => options.offset,
                            :sort => options.sort) do |id, score|
    doc = index[id]
    puts "%1.5f => %s" % [score, doc[:path]]
    options.fields.each do |field|
      puts "\t#{field} => #{doc[field]}" if doc[field]
    end
  end
  start = options.offset
  finish = [options.offset + options.limit, total].min
  puts "** #{start}-#{finish} of #{total} documents found **"
end
```

Now that we have all the code, we can take it for a spin. Here are some examples of how you would use it:

```
dave$ ferretfind -c -a "/path/to/documents/**/*" "/path/to/documents2/**/*"
dave$ ferretfind -a "/path/to/photos/**/*.{jpg,JPG,jpeg,JPEG}"
...
dave$ ferretfind -a "/path/to/documents3/**" -u
```

```
dave$ ferretfind -q "ruby and rails" -l 20 -o 20
dave$ ferretfind -q 'artist:"David Gray" album:"White Ladder"'
dave$ ferretfind -q "date_taken:>=20060601 comment:Tokyo" -s "date_taken DESC"
```

Summary

In this chapter, we built the start of what could be, with a little work, a very powerful PC search application. This is only a small example of what is possible with Ferret. We hope it has given you some ideas about how you can use Ferret to improve your current project or even just aid you in your day-to-day work life. Welcome to the Ferret community!

Index

We'd like to hear your suggestions for improving our indexes. Send email to *index@oreilly.com*.

M

N

O

P

Q

R

S

About the Author

David Balmain is a freelance software developer and the primary developer of the open source library Ferret. He gained an interest in high-performance text processing at university, where he earned a B.S. specializing in natural language processing. Recently, he has taken an interest in web application development and become enamored with the scripting language Ruby.

Colophon

The animal on the cover of *Ferret* is a ferret. The scientific name for the domestic ferret is *Mustela putorius furo*, or "weasel-like smelly thief." These slender, carnivorous mammals are about 20 inches long—including a 5-inch tail—weigh 2–4 pounds, and live for 7–10 years. Common colors include albino, chocolate, butterscotch, silver, and cinnamon. The domestic ferret is sometimes confused with the wild black-footed ferret (*Mustela nigripes*), an endangered North American mammal related to the Russian polecat. Male ferrets are called *hobs*, female ferrets are *jills*, and young ferrets are *kits*. A group of ferrets is a *business*.

Ferrets were first bred 2,500 years ago in Africa for hunting rabbits. Today they are more often kept as pets, and are now the third most popular pet in the United States after cats and dogs. Ferrets are intelligent and playful; they can recognize their names and learn simple tricks. They have a habit of stealing household objects and hiding them—socks, keys, books, umbrellas, T.V. remotes, even fish out of bowls. When ferrets are excited and want to play, they bounce and flop around in a routine known as a "weasel war dance." They may also hiss and arch their backs. Ferrets in war dances tend to be clumsy, often hopping into things or tripping on their own feet.

Some parts of the world restrict the keeping of ferrets. A ferret-free zone, or FFZ, is a place where ferrets are banned or illegal. Three reasons are often cited for a ban: ferrets may bite or scratch children; there is no proven rabies vaccine for ferrets; and ferrets may threaten native wildlife. However, these points are often disputed. Former mayor of New York City Rudy Giuliani infamously clashed with ferret lovers in 2001, when the city council considered dropping the ban on ferrets and Giuliani opposed it, railing against ferrets as "wild animals." Still, many regions are being persuaded to change their anti-ferret laws, and the only U.S. states that now ban ferrets are California and Hawaii.

The cover image is from the Dover Pictorial Archive. The cover font is Adobe's ITC Garamond. The text font is Linotype Birka, the heading font is Adobe Myriad Condensed, and the code font is LucasFont's TheSans Mono Condensed.